SLOAN DUPLOYAN SHORTHAND

BUSINESS LETTERS

Transcripted by: VINOD KUMAR

Notion Press

NOTION PRESS

India. Singapore. Malaysia.

ISBN xxx-x-xxxxx-xx-x

This book has been published with all reasonable efforts taken to make the material error-free after the consent of the author. No part of this book shall be used, reproduced in any manner whatsoever without written permission from the author, except in the case of brief quotations embodied in critical articles and reviews.

The Author of this book is solely responsible and liable for its content including but not limited to the views, representations, descriptions, statements, information, opinions and references ["Content"]. The Content of this book shall not constitute or be construed or deemed to reflect the opinion or expression of the Publisher or Editor. Neither the Publisher nor Editor endorse or approve the Content of this book or guarantee the reliability, accuracy or completeness of the Content published herein and do not make any representations or warranties of any kind, express or implied, including but not limited to the implied warranties of merchantability, fitness for a particular purpose. The Publisher and Editor shall not be liable whatsoever for any errors, omissions, whether such errors or omissions result from negligence, accident, or any other cause or claims for loss or damages of any kind, including without limitation, indirect or consequential loss or damage arising out of use, inability to use, or about the reliability, accuracy or sufficiency of the information contained in this book.

Edition: 2023

SLOAN DUPLOYAN SHORTHAND,

BUSINESS LETTERS

Author: Vinod Kumar

© No part of this book shall be used, reproduced in any manner whatsoever without written permission from the author, except in the case of brief quotations embodied in critical articles and reviews.

Disclaimer:

The Publisher and Editor shall not be liable whatsoever for any errors, omissions, whether such errors or omissions result from negligence, accident, or any other cause or claims for loss or damages of any kind, including without limitation, indirect or consequential loss or damage arising out of use, inability to use, or about the reliability, accuracy, inaccuracy or sufficiency, insufficiency of the information contained in this book.

ISBN:

This book is dedicated to my parents.

Contents

Class	Sections
General Letters	I to 6
Railway Letters	7 to 9
Shipping Letters	10 to 13
Engineering Letters	14 to 19
Legal Letters	20 to 25
Valuation Letters	26 to 28
Financial Letters	29 to 31
Note that the above figures denote Sections, and not Pages.	

(Before reading this 'Business Letters' book one must read the main book "SLOAN DUPLOYAN SHORTHAND" to understand the outlines of this stenography.). Here is the cover of the book.

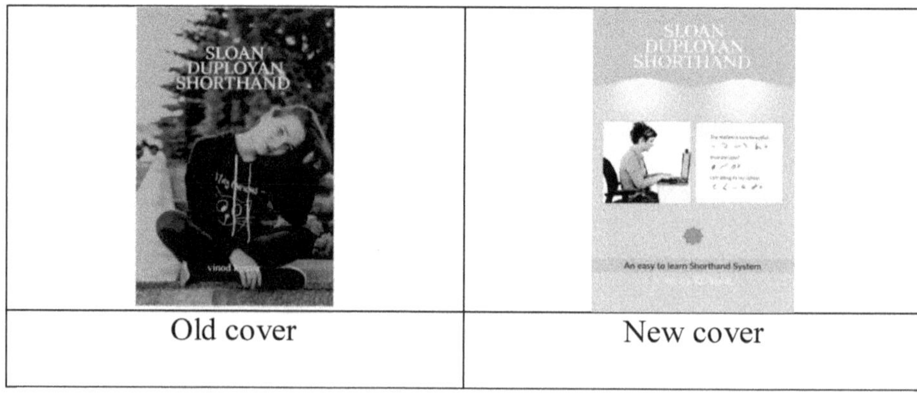

Old cover	New cover

Preface

Sloan Duployan Shorthand is a very simple English Shorthand learning system. Students can learn it in total 10 Sections of the book. The Sloan Duployan Shorthand book is available online.

This separate book- Business Letters is in continuation to the book Sloan Duployan Shorthand learning book. In this book Business letters are given in few Sections as an exercise and example. Students should practice these letters and pick up speed of their shorthand writing.

Students can be familiar with this shorthand system in 2-3 months of practice and can get writing speed with regular practice of the lessons.

Learn yourself with these books and teach at least one other student to make this easy shorthand system popular.

Vinod Kumar

Date: 26.3.2023

A FEW WORDS ON PHRASING

The normal principles of Sloan-Duployan result in such short and practical outlines that there is no need for the memorisation of lists of arbitrary special forms to represent phrases. It has been stated that while abbreviation is a necessity in other systems, it is a luxury in Sloan-Duployan.

The extent to which the luxury of abbreviation may be applied to phrasing is a matter of common sense. In this book will be found many examples of phrasing for which no instruction or rules have been given in the " Instructor " lessons. Common sense has been the guide throughout, and even beginners with an elementary knowledge of business phraseology should find it easy to get the idea of these abbreviated forms without special memorisation.

The following are some common examples of the method employed : " In-rep-to-your " will readily be recognised as " In reply to your." " W-refer-to-your " as " With reference to your." " In-regar-to-our " as " In regard to our." " Encl-pl-find " as " Enclosed please find." " We-are-rec-favour " as " We are in receipt of your favour."

It will be noticed that in phrases " b " has been used for " beg," and " ob " for " oblige." While these words should be written fully when standing alone it will be found safe to use the suggested abbreviation in a phrase. Note the examples : " We-b-thank-you " for " We beg to thank you." " We-b-to-remain " for " We beg to remain." " I-am-ob " for " I am obliged." " We-are-much-ob " for " We are much obliged."

Place names have been written in full, with the exception of abbreviated forms for London (L-un-un), Liverpool (L-vr-l), and Birmingham (Brum).

When we look in the past, we see that there was two main English Shorthand Systems developed in England. These were popular shorthand writing systems. One was Pitman Shorthand System, which is mostly people learn in India and abroad. Second one was Sloan Duployan Shorthand System. Second system of shorthand was famous in India till 70's and many students learnt it and got jobs in Govt./Private organisations.

I found this old book written in Sloan Duployan Shorthand. In this book 'Business Letters' was written in Shorthand only. I tried to transcribe it in English. As no teacher and guidance is available to me to transcribe it in English, I tried my best for transcribing it in English. There may be some errors and mistakes somewhere but it will be very helpful in reading and understanding the outlines of the shorthand book. By practicing it you can recognise the outlines and increase your knowledge and shorthand speed.

One must have to understand what Shorthand is. Shorthand is a short outline for a word or for a phrase. You can make your own outline for a word or phrase and read it for the same word or phrase. The shorthand purpose completes.

Learn these outlines of shorthand. Make yourself an expert of this shorthand and develop some outline for your own. When you get this shorthand learnt, and then please teach at least one person to promote this shorthand system so that it can gain its popularity again.

It is very easy to learn and one can get speed in short duration. (This book has some shorthand outlines circled with pencil and a suggested outline is provided at side by the old user that can be helpful so it is not removed.)

-Vinod Kumar

1.

25 — 26

30

1.

James Anderson Esquire, Lincoln (UK)

Dear Sir, In reply to your enquiry of yesterday date we have pleasure in enclosing our catalogue of house furniture. Our speciality is the royal top desk described on pages 25 and 26 and we venture to think that this article will meet your requirements exactly being of good workmanship convenient for design and moderate in price.   Any further information that you may desire, we shall be most happy to supply.   Hoping to be favour with your esteem comments. we are dear sir,   Yours faithfully,

W B Alanson Esquire, Canterbury (UK)

Dear Sir, we acknowledge with accent the receipt of your letter of 7th instant (current month) containing order for a six unit quarter and all on bookcase which is receiving our best attention. The case is now being packed and will be ready for dispatch par rail tomorrow 9th inst. (Instant=Current month).   Enclosed please find proforma invoice and we shall be glad to have remittance at your earliest convenience. Thanking you in anticipation, we are yours truly.

C. Trainer Esquire, Swansea. (Wales)

Dear Sir, We are receiver of 30th ult. (Ultimo=Previous month) and in reply I would say that

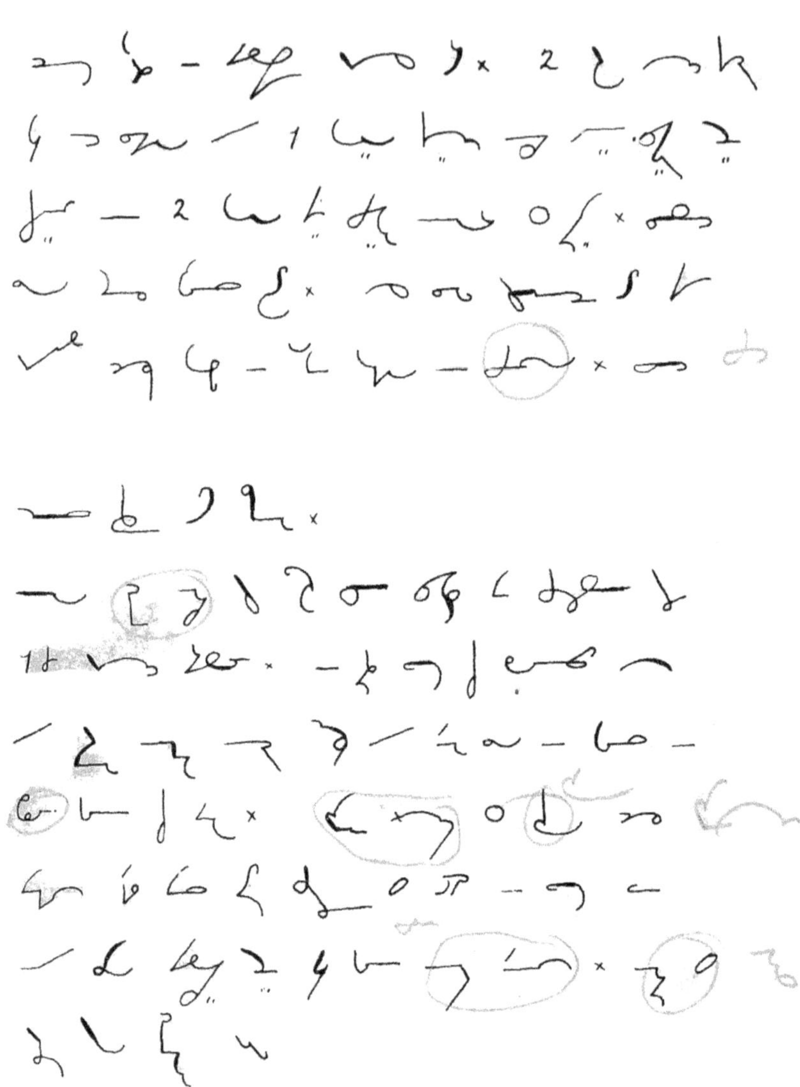

§ 2.

we do not manufacture these class of goods for which you have enquired. 2 firms which we believe make these articles are 1. M/s Beeching and Co. Ltd. Hollygrave Street Bolton and 2. M/s John Colmin and Sons of Waging. A tier of these houses no doubt would meet your requirements. Shall you at any future date require goods in our line? We shall be most happy to submit samples and quotations. Yours truly

Andrew Boyd Esquire Aberdeen. (Scotland)UK

Dear Sir, we beg to thank you for your esteemed order of this morning with postal order value one pound for which we are enclosing receipt. The packing returned by you has duly reached in our forwarding department and we have instructed our counting house to remit you the amount paid by you on the same. With reference to the exchange of bases/cases we shall with pleasure comply with your request provide you to undertake the return it to our warehouse Glasgow Street carriage paid and in good condition. Thanking you,

for past various we beg to remain, Yours faithfully.

2.

M/s Barnet and Chandelier Manchester.   Dear Sirs we beg to acknowledge the receipt of your order dated 16th Instant but regret

that we cannot now supply these goods at the terms on which we have fulfilled previous orders. The operations of certain capitalists on the other side of the Atlantic have resulted in a corner and a consequent rapid rise in the market. Please let us know whether we may fulfil your order at the increased rate of 2 pence per piece over and above that of your last order.   Yours faithfully

M/s Dunlop and Sons, Ardrossan (UK)

Dear Sirs, In reply to your favour of 18th instant we are sending you by tonight's post, Pens as per invoice enclosed together with statement from which we have deducted the additional discount as arranged. We are afraid, it will be quite impossible for us to put your name on the pens unless you can give us a stock order. We shall be pleased to do anything possible we can, to assist you in the sale and trust that it will be possible for you to send us an order to enable us to exceed to your request. Yours faithfully

The John and Williams Co. New York.

Gentlemen, your favour of the 21st December carry tend duly and we discovered today that by some oversight it has not been acknowledged. We beg to apology for this delay

83.

and to say that we shall be pleased to take up the question of handling your goods in England and shall write to you fee in the matter, in the course of a few days.   Thanking you,

For considering us, we are, Yours Truly

Albert Bark Esquire, South Sea

Dear Sirs, With reference to your letter of the 2nd instant regarding "Book of songs", we are not aware that the letter of Greek stands upon which the contents of this book were originally drawn are your property. At any rate we have had to make up fresh systems at our own expense on the last occasion that we had your order in. Under these circumstances we have not delivered the systems to your messenger who called today. We are dear sir, Yours Faithfully

3. R.S. Tailor Esquire, Belfast (UK)

Dear Sir, We have your letter authorising us to proceed to the execution of your order of October 15 last and beg to assure you that the same will have our very prompt attention. Our Mills are all running on full time and the force now employed is greater than we have ever had engaged at one time. This is because large orders have been coming in so rapidly that it will require more than our full capacity to full fill them

on time. Not with this the first shipment upon your order will be made on December 15 which we trust will be satisfactory to you.

Thanking you for past favours we are dear sir, Yours truly

C. L. Paterson's Esquire, London S.E.

Dear Sir, we are under the necessity of informing you that owing to a series of misfortunes during the last few months we find it not in our part to meet our engagements and we are consequently induced to submit our affairs to the inspection of our parent's creditors. We request you to immediately furnish to assignee Mister W J Gaid with an abstract of your account current for the purpose of having it compared with our books in order that to carry on balance may be ascertained. Your obedient servants

Edward young Esquire, Coventry (UK).

Dear Sir I am obliged by your letter of May 26 with reference to terms of the "Commercial Dictionary". It will of course give me great pleasure to see you doing a good business with this publication by the time you asked for the best terms and point out that you are in a somewhat different position from that of the ordinary retailer who merely

§ 4.

supplies a demand I would refer you to the fact that I have already given you different terms. I am charging you 1 shilling each whereas the ordinary retailor piece 1 / 2. I cannot charge you less than 1 shilling for the book which is as you are aware issued as a net publication. I hope we may have the advantage of your cooperation in the sale of the book because the benefit will certainly be a mutual one. Yours faithfully.

4.

M/s Mathew Gardener and Sons, Ashton-under-Lyne, (Greater Manchester, England)

Dear Sirs, Herewith I have handed you a cheque value 72 pound 10 shillings for settlement of enclosed account. Kindly acknowledge the receipt and oblige. With reference to my order of the 8th ult. (ultimo) which you promised to fulfil by the 15th of this month, a week has now elapsed since the appointed date and the goods have not yet come to this end. The delay has caused me great inconvenience and I am loosing orders all most daily. Please push forward with the execution of my order with all despatch and forward at least a portion of the goods tomorrow certainly to reach me by Thursday. Yours truly.

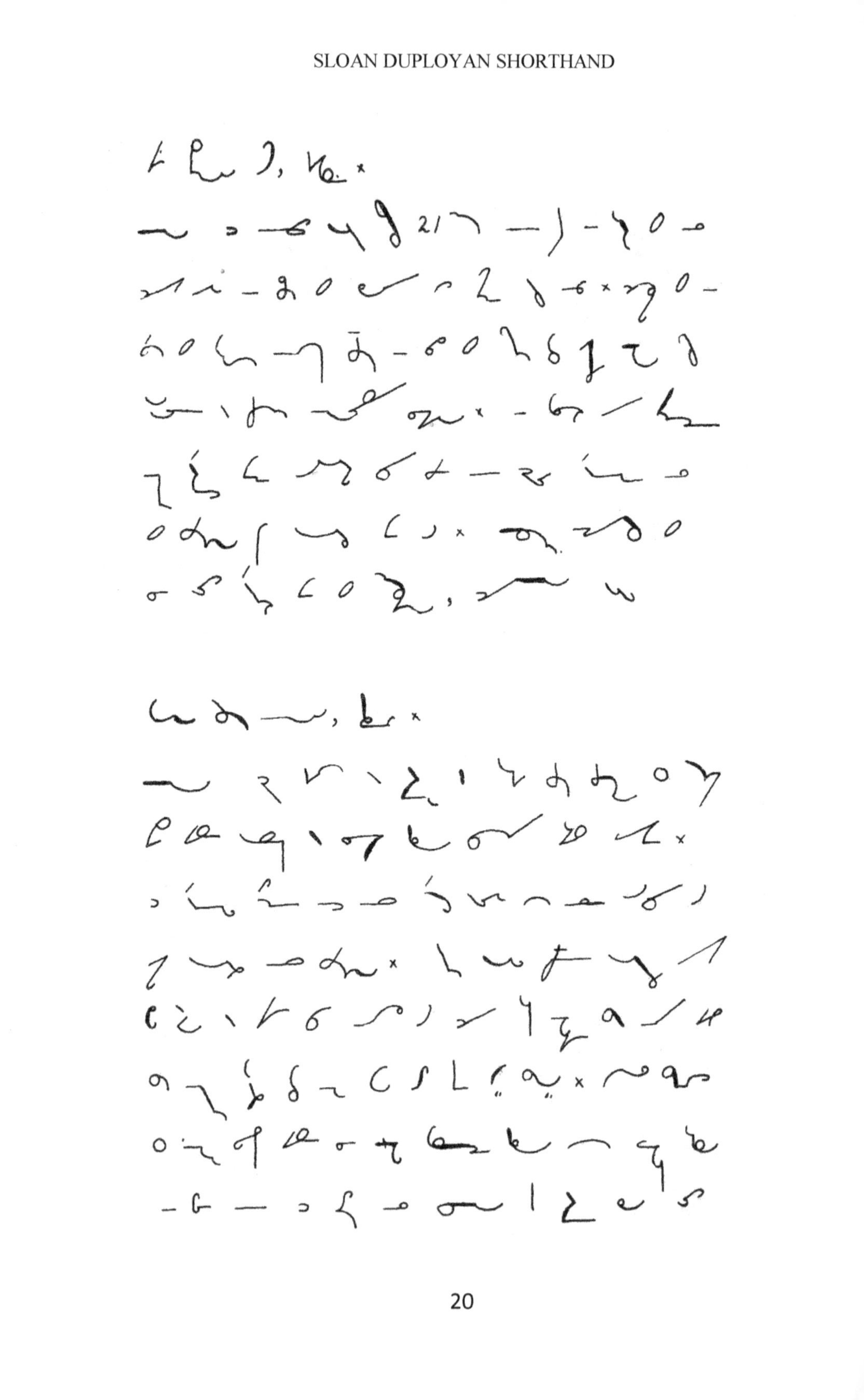

John Robinson Esquire, Plymouth (England)

Dear Sir, we have duly received your favour of 21st instant and beg to inform you that we are quite willing to appoint you as our only agent in your town. We shall give you the commission you mentioned and should be disposed to allow you even more liberal terms if you succeed in pushing the sale of our articles. The machines are granted to be in conformity with the specifically all our catalogue and we feel confident that your customers would be satisfied with them. Trusting to hear from you at early convenience with your instructions, we are Dear Sir, Yours faithfully

M/s Foster and Sons, Brighton (England)

Dear Sirs, We have pleasure in forwarding pair sample post patterns of strong oval cloth suitable for hardware prices of which are enclosed herewith. We confidently recommend these to your consideration feeling sure that their superior quality will give satisfaction to your customers. Having recently executed several large army contracts for goods of this special quality we are enable to make this offer to our clients owing to having manufacture more than it was required by the Ware House. This is an opportunity of obtaining reliable cloth at extremely moderate prices which it may be impossible to repeat and we request that orders be forwarded as early

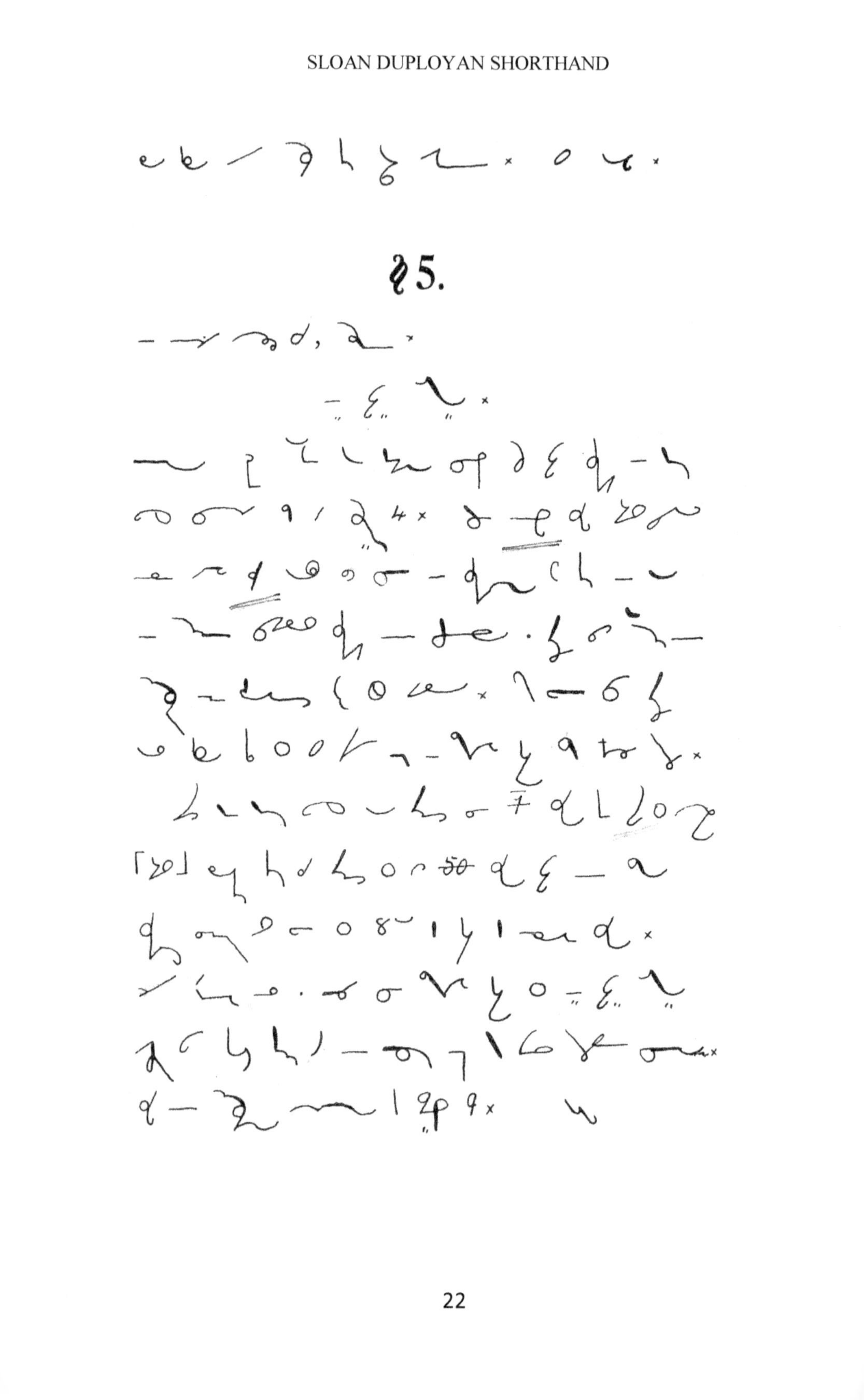

¶ 5.

as possible our stock being somewhat limited. Yours Sincerely.

5.

The Dell China Co., Stafford (England)

The weekly universe

Dear Sirs, we beg to submit some particulars of that by a new weekly publication, the first issue of which will appear on November 4. From the dummy copy enclosed. You will see that the literary crack is of a high order to publishers aim being to raise the standard of this class of publication and produce a journal highly interesting and instructive to the present day men of all classes. Every reader of this journal is a possible about all your goods; therefore the advertising pages offer exceptional value.

Circulation for the first issue is guaranteed at 100000 copies but the circular of charges (enclosed) has been based on a guarantee of only 50000 copies weekly and offers publicity at the very low rate of 8 shillings per page per thousand copies. We are confident that a trial of the advertising pages of 'The Weekly Universe' will prove its business bringing quality and trust to be favour with your valued orders. Copy and instructions should reach us by October 9. Yours faithfully

M/s Keen and Sons, London, W.

Dear Sirs, In reply to your postcard regarding "Careers" we have the pleasure to send you a syllabus of the first 3 numbers as the proprietors are not agree by the issue information any further in advance contracting that. You will note from the original circular that we are not accepting advertisement for letting the first 3 numbers and if you wish to appear in these we should hear by Monday morning as we are going to Paris Tuesday with the first part. M/s W H Smith and sons have placed a larger order for "Careers" then they have given for any previous fortnightly part and instead of a management of 150000 of the first part we are anticipating almost double. There is very little advertising space available so we shall be glad to hear from you if you want to appear. Yours faithfully

The Cloud Motor Co. Coventry (England)

Gentlemen(see 125 page of SDS) we are acting as the representatives in Great Britain of the international exhibition to be held next year and have instructions from the executive to answer your letter addressed to the chief office. We must inform you that an early application for space is of paramount importance, as the area allotted to this country is necessarily limited and a large portion has been already taken up.

including all packing and insurance as I buy for the sum of 60 Guineas (sixty Guineas){currency of England 1 Guineas =1.05 Pound}. Otherwise the price to send down specially on an earlier date, as we have nothing else to fit in at the moment -- would be 70 Guineas (seventy Guineas) for the motor paint kit and trailer are 85 Guineas (eighty five Guineas) for 2 single vehicles; and our main task includes all unfixing and re-fixing of the furniture Bed Studs etc. As the offer for the 19th and 20th September is subject to the availability of vehicles still being disengaged. We are enclosing a prepaid wear for your reply as this would save disappointment. Yours faithfully.

Francis White Esq, Manchester (England)

Dear Sir, regarding new import duties, the attention of the Executive Council of this Trades Federation of Great Britain and Ireland has been drawn to certain statements which have appeared in the press as to the effect the revised duties on machines and parts will have on the trade in general and enclosed in particular. These statements they have reason to believe, will be difficult if not impossible to substantiate. This Council has also been informed that certain irresponsible communications have also been issued which they feel will have detrimental effects.

upon future negotiations with A M Gover. The executive council has had this matter well in the end and trust they have dealt diplomatically with the situation and so that you should be familiar with what has taken place. They have decided unanimously to send those interested in the trade a resume of what has taken place officially and this has happened here too. You will find enclosed a copy of the import duty report which I trust will give you a real grasp of the situation. That, you may fully realise the importance of this Trades Federation of Great Britain and Ireland. I am instructed to state that its members are drawn from:

1.   Wholesale and retail dealers

2.   Importers of parts

3.   British Manufacturers

4.   Agents for a marking Machines

5.   Agents for continental machines

6.   Manufacturers of accessories

I also enclose an application form for membership and suggest this is an opportunity time for you to give and obtain support to the official organisation of your own trade. Yours faithfully.

27.

7.

The Goods Agent, Ostium Station, London.

Dear Sir, we have dispatched from Manchester tonight 34 bales Linen consigned to M/s Selfridges, Oxford State, London.

This consignment is extremely urgent and we shall be obliged if you will arrange to deliver as early as possible tomorrow. We have also sent today a fairly large quantity of bales for our own London. Address at low Times Street. Most of the goods dispatched today are for Christmas sale and this is absolutely essential that delivery be made before noon tomorrow. We trust you will again favour us with special delivery.   Yours faithfully.

The Goods Agent, St. Pancras Station, London

Dear Sir, we intercept using a service of containers commences about the end of this month for the conveyance of certain lines of our goods for delivery to our Goswell Road address and on preparing parliamentary arrangements. We find that it will only be suitable for our Goswell Road people to have these unloads at their premises at 8 AM each morning. We were wondering therefore

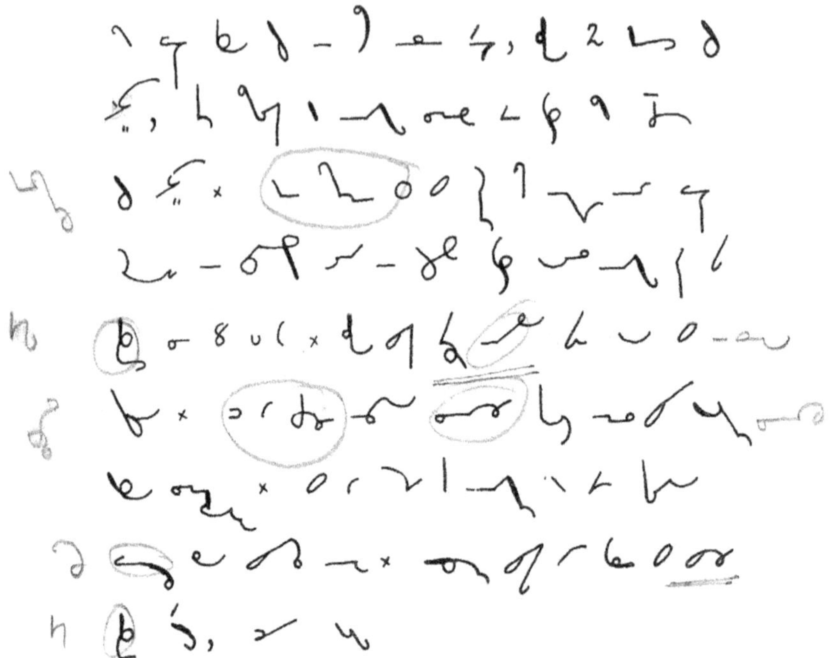

if it would be possible for you to arrange that the containers, perhaps 2 per day from Leeds (UK town), being available for delivery at that time in the morning after dispatch from Leeds. In the event of you are not being able to have this done. It would be necessary to hold over until the following morning so that delivery could be given promptly at 8 AM (see page 113 of Sloan dup shorthand instructor). Perhaps you will be good enough to write to us giving your views. We would point out that this is additional business that you are receiving from us at the present time. You would still be delivering in quantity bales, etc., as you are now doing. Trusting you will give this matter to your usual prompt consideration, we are, Yours faithfully

M/s Curey Hovending and Sons. 'Leeds'

Dear Sir, I am the receiver of the 16th instant respecting containers and beg to inform you that the train from 'Leeds' is only through here at 5:30 AM by providing the goods reach here within a few minutes of scheduled time, I think we shall be able to deliver by 8 AM as requested. I take it that if a tender was made a few minutes after this time delivery would be taken. I note that in the event of the train being late, delivery should be made on the following morning and I am taking up the

28.

matter with the Leeds agent with a view to sign that the containers are wired forwarder so that my people can make the necessary arrangements as regards to delivery. Yours faithfully.

8.

The District Manager, Great western Railway Gloucester (England)

Dear Sir,

At the end of September a consignment consisting of a walnut barrow was sent from Naroj to M/s G S Tailor, loan cottage, Stroud (District in England), and was found to be damaged on arrival at that address. I believe M/s Tailor had the matter discussed with you Mr Temple and that an offer was made of settlement for 8/6 being the cost of repair. There is however, one further point I would like to mention with regard to the damage and replacement of leg that to barrow, which is an antique one and of some value, has depreciated in value owing to the replacement part not being of the same date as the original furniture. I think some consideration should be made by you people for loss and I have now to intimate a claim of 3 pounds to cover this. I hope to hear from you soon regarding settlement. Yours faithfully.

The Goods Manager, Marylebone Station, London.

Dear Sir,

We have handed over to your Glasgow High Street Station today 70 bales and one box addressed to M/s Fuller Castle and Sons ltd. Johnson's Court Fleet street London. They have gone par to One Day Service and we trust you will make arrangements for delivery being made to that address early tomorrow morning. We are testing right this service with your company and ensure that it will be satisfactory. We hope to give you fairly big consignments every Friday from Glasgow. Would you be good enough to let us know whether you could guarantee us regular deliveries early every Saturday morning. With many thanks, we are, Yours truly

M/s Stevens Gilmore and Co., Glasgow.

Dear Sirs,

With reference to your favour of 9th instant respecting 70 bales and one box. I regret to inform you that the Scotch Train on which your Goods were dispatched do not arrive here until 9.56 AM. On Saturday after which the placing of the wagons had to be carried out and it was found that we were unable to carry out delivery on Saturday morning, But we telephoned your London office in regard to the position and promised delivery on this morning which was done. It is very difficult

29.

to see whether delivery in all cases can be made on Saturday Mornings, everything depending on the time of arrival. However, if you will advise us the time of despatching on Fridays everything possible shall be done here to clear in the morning of arrival. Yours Truly.

9.

M/s Hubert Sons Ltd, Edinburgh (UK)

Dear Sirs, In connection with the parcels which are passing via the L N E Railway Company and the LMS Railway Company. Some of these dispatches will be taken place through the Christmas period and we should like to make different arrangements in respect of the same. It is of course our desire to avoid sending the parcels by post but to enable us to decide whether this will be unnecessary we would like you to obtain from the respective Railway companies a different date up to which they will receive parcels and guarantee delivery before Christmas. We think this is very essential especially in view of the extra traffic which is bound to be on rail at that time and might interfere with the normal services. At the moment it looks that the average time for a parcel to reach its destination is about four days. As soon as you ascertain the date which they consider allows them submissioning on time for handling to ensure the delivery we can make

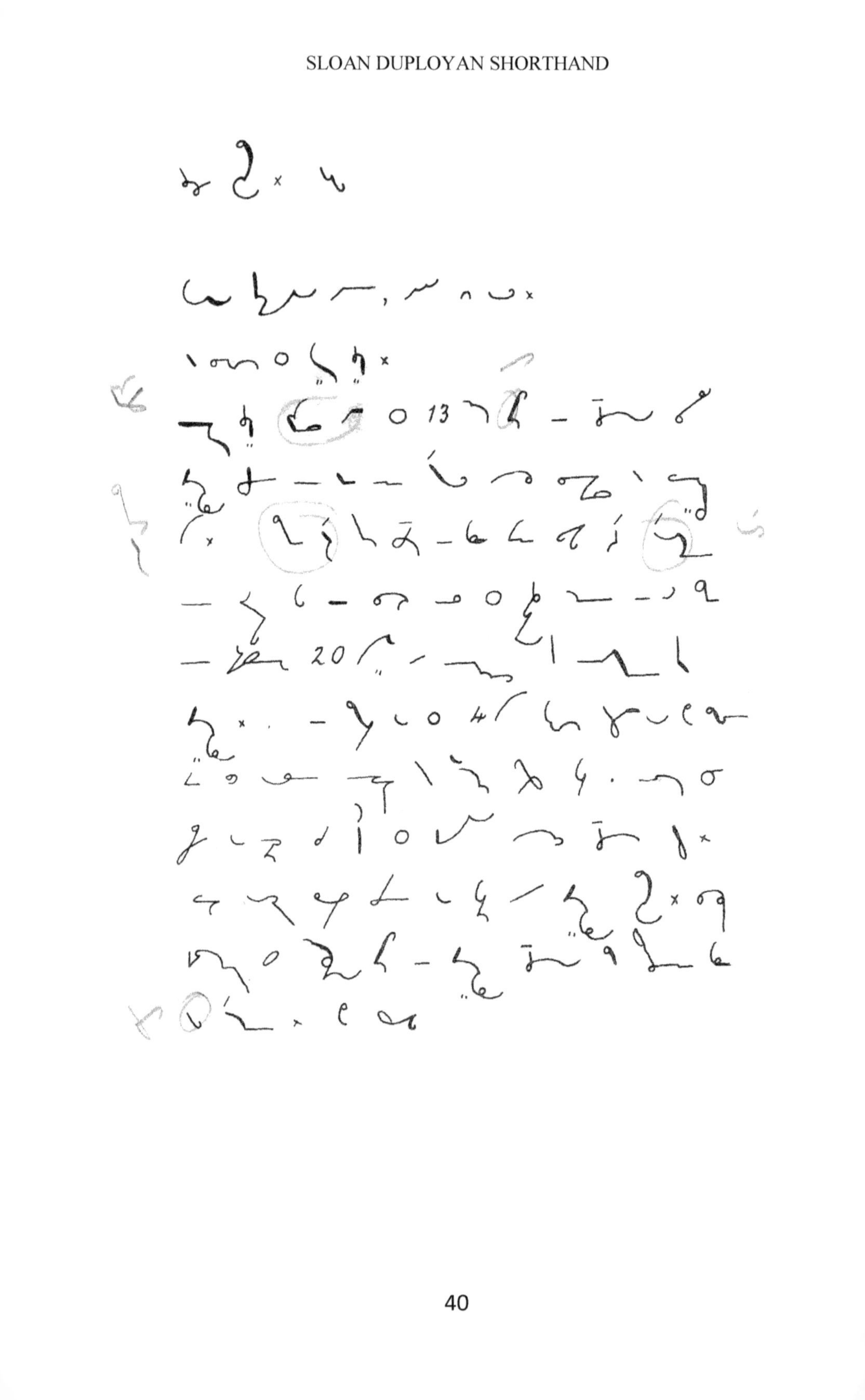

final arrangements. Yours faithfully.

M/s Barinksels Ltd, London EC

For the attention of Mr Piper.

Dear Mr Piper with reference to your letter of 13th instant regarding the dispatches around Christmas period and further to the conversation which I had with you in Eden Borough days. I have to confirm having discussed the matter with the railway companies concerned and they have given me their assurance that all packages handed to them up to and including 20th December will definitely be delivered before Christmas. The average time of 4 days mentioned in your letter so I am afraid on the high side and it would be very interesting if you could make a test of the actual time taken on a number of parcels which we dispatched for you.

It would serve as a good guide time making our Christmas arrangements. I shall be pleased to have your instructions regarding the Christmas dispatches after you have had the matter fully considered. I am, Yours sincerely.

§ 10.

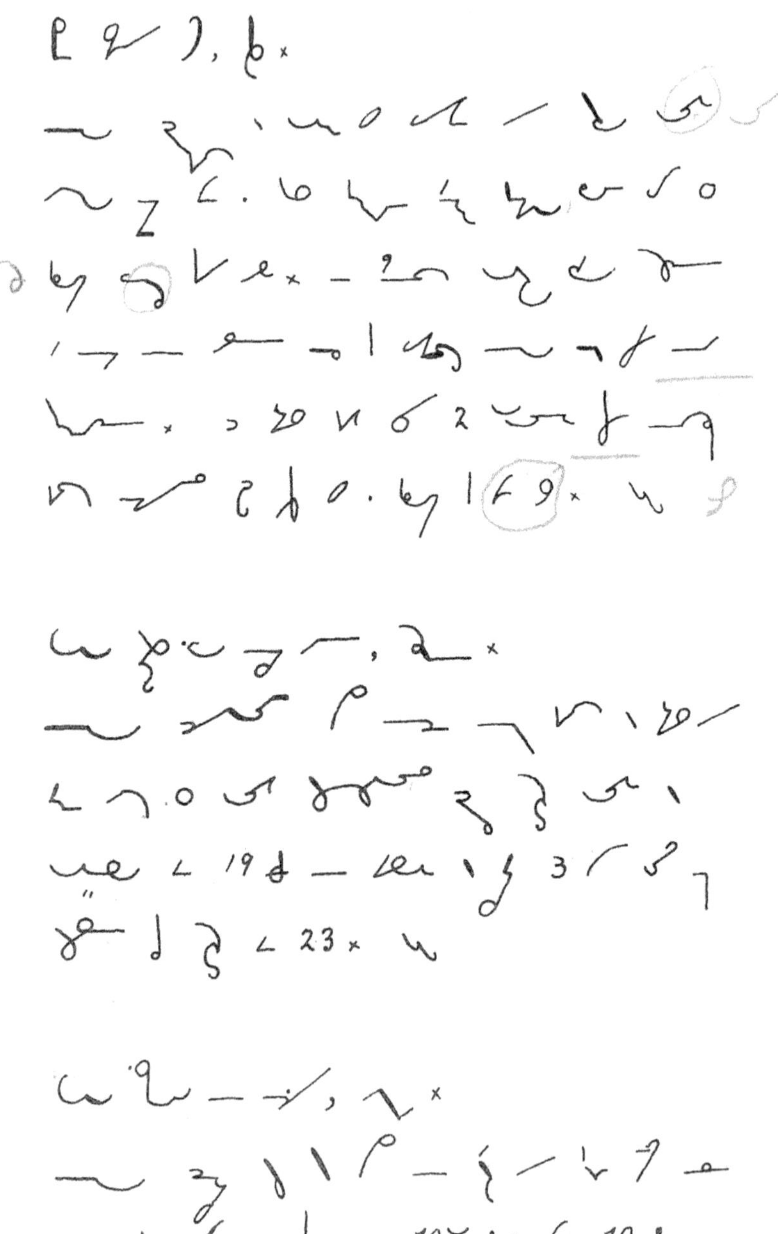

10

Hobart Okuner Esquire, Bromwich (England)

Dear Sir, We have pleasure in sending you herewith our various selling lists together with a small pamphlet containing particulars as the rates of passage etc. by our line. The accommodation is in most cases situated on deck and lighted throughout by electricity and is therefore cool and well ventilated. We are enclosing plans of our 2 succeeding boats and shall be pleased to hear that we may book you a passage by one of them. Yours faithfully

M/s Faulkner Haise and co. ltd, Stanford

Dear Sirs, We are in receipt of the letter of yesterday date and have pleasure in enclosing our current list of selling's from which you will see that we have a steamer sailing for Centos on the 19th approx. and closing for cargo 3 days earlier to be followed by a steamer on the 23rd . Yours faithfully

M/s Hobsons and Tailor, Liverpool

Dear Sirs, We thank you for your favour of yesterday and confirm our telephone message that the rate on smooth ware to Bunauser is 10 shillings per ton with 10 percent

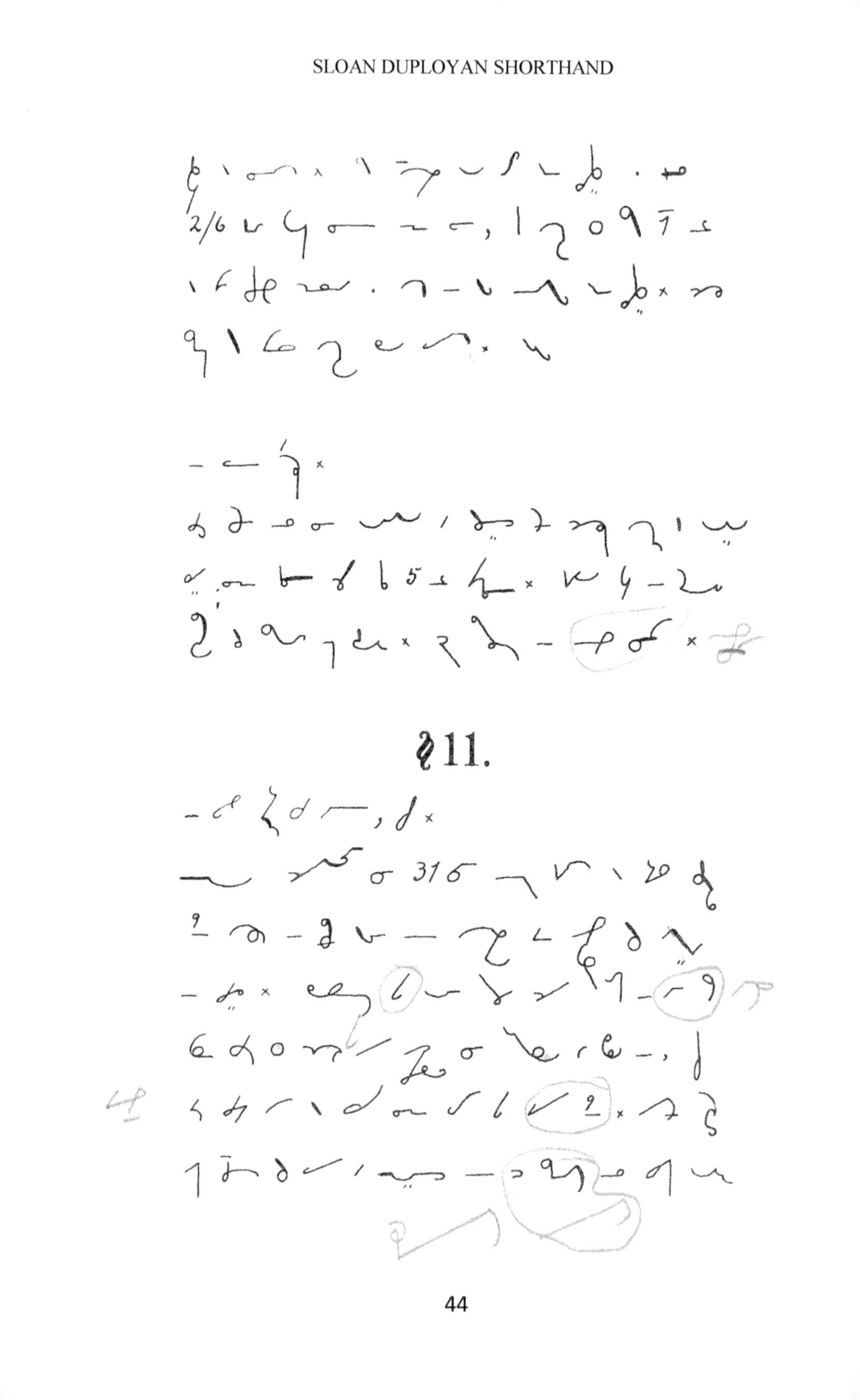

§11.

primage in addition. If discharge is required in the Boca an extra 2/6 per ton must be added to the rate, but shipment of over 100 tons in one bottom entitles a shipper to free delivery in the Boka. We shall hope to be favoured with your shipments as heretofore. Yours faithfully.

The Head Constable

Kindly note that at summers on Friday next we shall be shipping per Sais Royal at the powder grounds about 5 tons gunpowder. Please make the necessary arrangements for an officer to be present. We have advised the dock authorities.

11.

The Reliance Engineering Co. Ltd, Crewe (UK)

Dear Sirs,

We are in receipt of your letter of the 31st ult. (ultimo) and have pleasure in enclosing a proforma account showing the approx. freight and charges on the locomotive from Liverpool to Calau. As you do not give us the value, we are unable to let you know what cost of insurance or legalisation of the invoice would amount to, but you can collect this for yourself at the rates given on our account. Our next steamer will be despatched from here on Thursday and we hope to learn that you will be sending

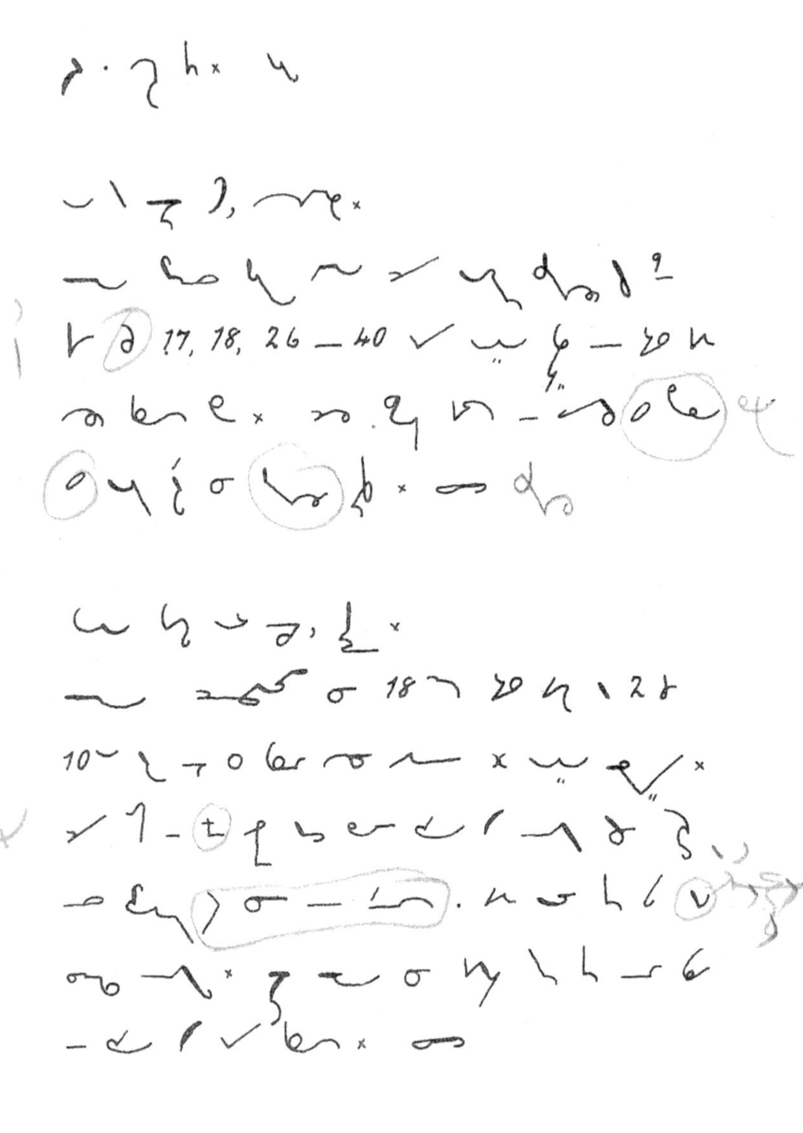

forward a shipment berry. Yours faithfully.

S V Darwin Esquire, Cheltenham

Dear Sir,

Referring to your previous letters we are reserving provisionally for your account boards number 17, 18, 26 and 40 in our SS Magic and enclose plan showing position of the same. We shall of course be pleased to hear from you as soon as you receive confirmation of the provisional booking. Yours Truly.

M/s Millionaire Sons and Co. Barkingside (UK)

Dear Sirs,

We duly received your letter of 18th inst.(instant) enclosed claim for 2 pound 10 shillings for some tens of motum short land. SS traveller. We are unable to accept liability for these as the cases were delivered from the steamer to your representative in good order and condition. A claim receipt being given for them at the time of delivery. There were no traces of the pilferage having been done while the cases were in our position. Yours Truly.

§12.

12.

M/s Reseal Barges and co. Braham (England)

Dear Sirs, We hereby beg to advise you that the under mentioned goods are held in our customs warehouse pending receipt of your instruction regarding clearance. We shall be pleased to establish and pass the necessary entries and the effect clearance through the customs on your behalf for such purpose we require the following documents and information:

(1) original invoice and copy. Where ad valorem (as per price) duty is payable to invoices must show charges paid for freight insurance and packing. If not shown on the invoice the import must declare on the invoice that the value indicated is CIF and or produce evidence of these values. We would advise you to carefully verify invoice particulars before sending them to ourselves for entry purposes and to indicate endeavour possible the tariff under which declaration is to be made on your behalf.

(2) Remittance covering the amount of duty made payable to us. If perfect and entry or the invoices in duplicate and form of authority are not received within 10 days the senders will be advised and will also be requested to agree to the return of the goods after 28 days of their arrival, if settle could end un-cleared. After the period of 10 days rental charges will be incurred. Dutiable goods which are required to be

warehoused in bond can be transferred to a bonded warehouse for your account. We are dear Sirs, Yours faithfully.

M/s R D and Co. London E

Dear Sirs,

We are in receipt of your advice of the 23rd instant reference B-2018 regarding 2 parcels of gold leaf. J. calf men on our account. We are enclosing herewith form C105 duly completed together with original and copy invoice and cheque for 21 pound in favour of H M Jostens for payment of duty. We shall be pleased if you will arrange early customs clearance and send it to us immediately thereafter. Yours faithfully

M/s Denson and Sons, Liverpool.

Dear Sirs, We are enclosing herewith through bill of lading in original and copy invoice with specification and form C105 duly completed for 31 bales prepared par to SS Whiteland to you in Liverpool today. We are also enclosing a cheque in favour of H M Jostens amounting to 9 pound 17/1 being the amount of duty liable on these goods. We shall be pleased if you will arrange for early customs clearance and deliver to our Waterloo (Canada) address. Yours truly

¶ 13.

7/6

20   8   6/9   8   14/3

275   4082

105

88 14/3

13.

Mr. Charls in Harson, Solair.

Dear Sir, Please note that we are advised of one box containing

Cotton block shipped to you for your account from Chicago L,. Steamer Majestic now in port, with the following charges: customs opening and clearance dues cartage etc. 7/6 duty 20 per cent 8 pound 6/9 (6 shillings 9 pence) totalling 8 pound 14/3. All goods detained by customs are otherwise are at unrise risk and expense. Please return the attached forms together with shipper's invoice. Yours truly.

The Ad marketing Express Co., Southampton (England)

Dear Sirs, I have your advice of the 27th ult. (ultimo) reference Y 4082 advising me of the arrival of one parcel containing a cotton block per SS Majestic. I regret that I have not **yet** received the supplier's invoice for the goods in question and I am therefore unable to give you the necessary details required on form C105. Unfortunately the goods in question are extremely urgent and are required immediately by my works department. I am therefore, sending you herewith a cheque in your name for 8 pound 14/3 (14 shillings 3 pence) in respect of duty to your clearance fees and also letter of authority for you to act as my agent. Is it possible for you now to have the goods cleared of customs?

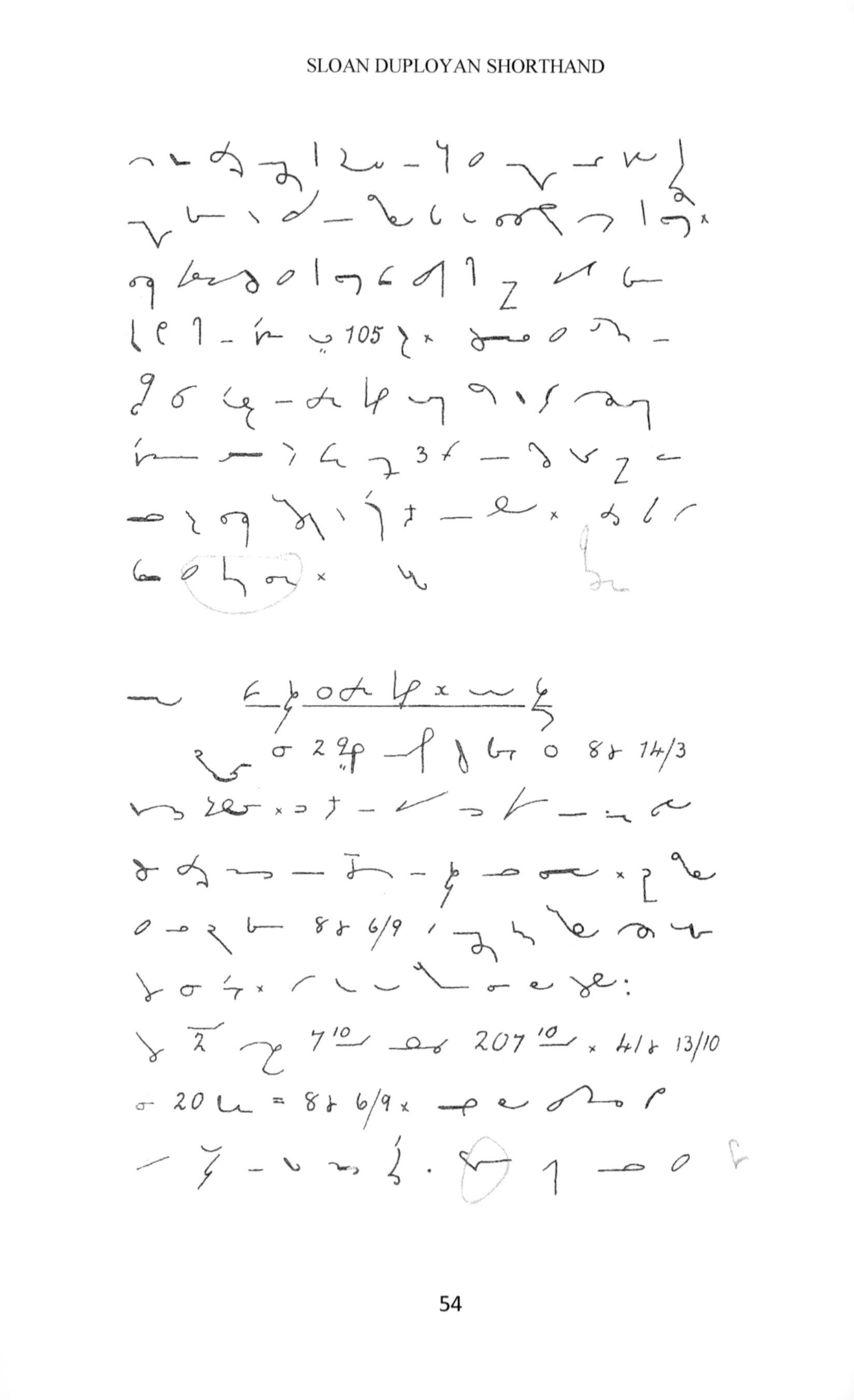

should further customs deposit be necessary to enable you to have this done please be good enough to have this paid in yourself and advise me in time I shall let you have the cheque be returned. I shall be glad to hear from you in return whether you will be able to get clearance made before I am able to complete C-105 form. In order to that you understand the urgency of this consignment the cotton block is to be used for work which has to be completed under contract within the next 3 weeks and if I fail to get it through in time I shall be involved in considerable expense and losses. Kindly give this matter your best attention. Yours faithfully

Dear Sir, One package of cotton block x SS Majestic We have received a letter of the 2nd October and will be obliged for your remittance of 8 pound 14/3 (14 sh. 3 p.) for which we have enclosed the receipt. We expect to clear these goods and obtain release from the customs today and dispatch the package to your address. We beg to advise you that we have paid 8 pound 6/9 on deposit pending invoice showing separate value of the containers. This sum is arrived at as follows:

Value 200 dollar, charges 7.10 dollars total 207.10 dollars. 41 pound 13/10 at 20 percent= 8 pound 6/9. Drawing as you are no doubt aware our subject to free entry consequently a refund will be due to you

§ 14.

best at 20 percent of the value of the drawing. We shall, therefore, be glad if you will please obtain an invoice from the shippers with the required information in order that we may have the deposit assessed. Yours truly.

14.

The Gresons Engineering Co. Derby (England)

Dear Sirs, One of your oil engines has been in regular use at this firm for about 6 years and so for it has needed to have little attention to our expenses for repairs. During the past few weeks, it has given much trouble but session to run without any cause which can be traced by the Forman was charge oil. I would like you to send one of your men to Hillside Firm before the end of the present month to put the engine into proper repair before bad weather sets in. A breakdown after the stocks are raised for the winter would be a very serious matter as I think the engine is used to drive the machines which crush the turnips and all this is required to feed over 100 head/herd of cattle. Perhaps you had better in the first instance send a man to examine the engine and see what difficulty is then one bearing with him afterwards everything necessary to make a thorough job. Please let me know on what day he will arrive and also the time

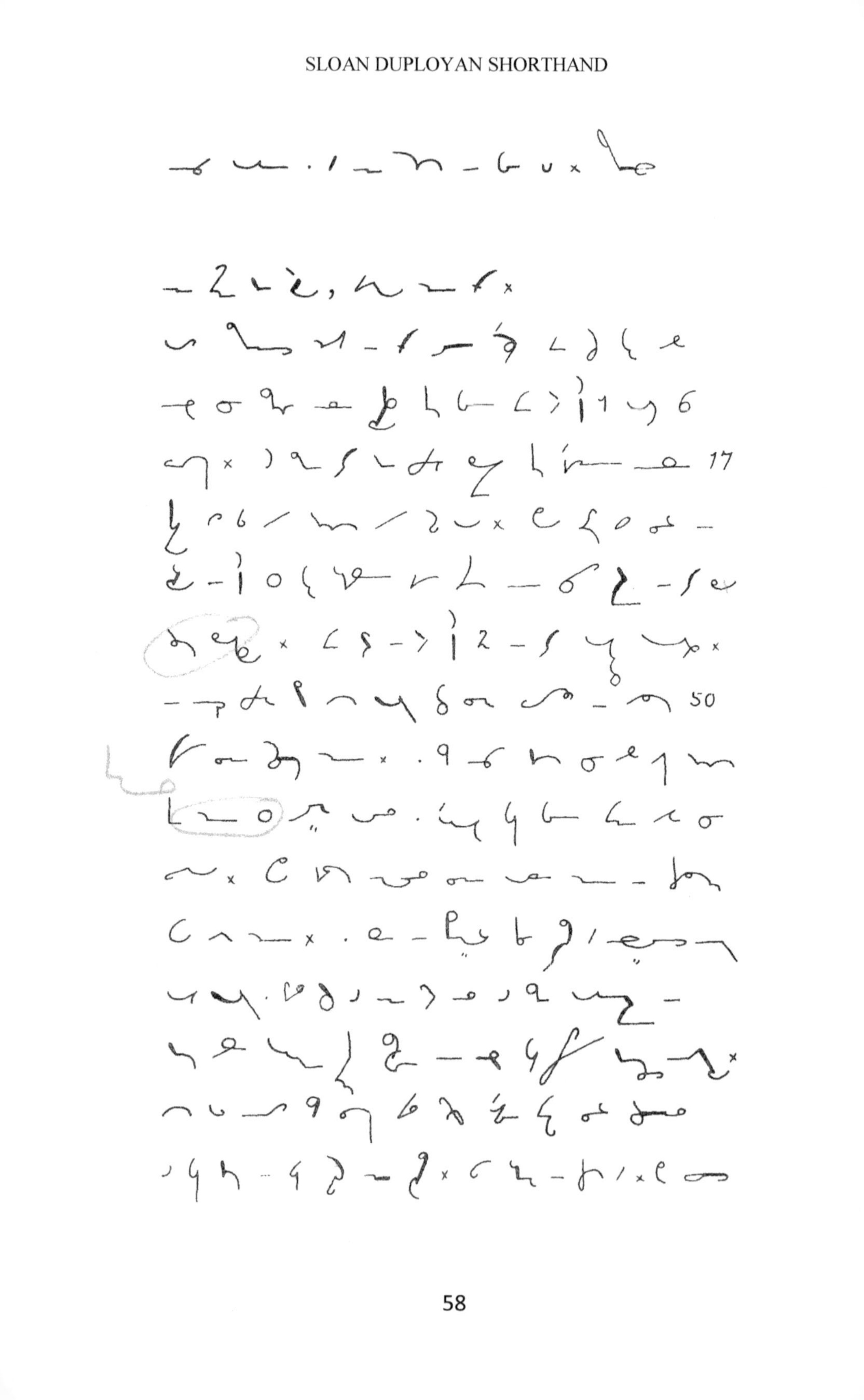

and I will send a car to the station to meet him. You have yours truly

To the Agent for the Contractors, Cliffs end Works

Sir, I have today inspected the works under construction on the new main line and I am of the opinion that the progress been made with contract number 1 is not what it should be. Not half of the work in the cottons has yet been completed and of the 17 bridges only 6 are finished or near so. I must request you at once to increase the number of men employed on this section and push forward the work as fast as possible. With reference to contract number 2, the work is much more satisfactory. The deep coting however should receive more attention especially the last 50 yards at the northern end. I hope that this portion of the line will be finished by the end of September so that a commencement may be made with the line of the rails. I was pleased to see that at the south end the ballasting was well in the end. I wrote to Robertsons about the iron work on Tuesday and have since received a reply from them to the effect that they hope to send forward the first lot of cement in the beginning of next month and thereafter make regular fortnightly deliveries. If any delay occurs, I shall be glad if you would communicate with me at once in order that they may be pressed to keep strictly to their agreement. It is important to push on. I am yours truly.

¶ 15.

15.

The Town Clerk, Newton on that time

Dear Sir, we beg to thank you for your letter of the 4th instant advising us that our tender for the reconstruction of a double track bridge at Newton has been accepted. The bridge is to be to our alternative plate girder design and we confirm that the lump sum price for the work will be 3945 pound which includes the sum of 300 pound to be regarding manning as a contingency item for extra work arising out of our extension to the present contract if ordered in line and certified by the engineer. The copy of the specification was returned with our tender and shall be much obliged if you will let us have a copy of it. The drawing referred to in your letter has not yet been received by us and we shall be glad to have a copy of it. Assuring you of our best attention we are Dear Sir, Yours faithfully.

Dear Sirs, Contract number 294. Reconstruction of Railway Bridge. I send herewith in duplicate formal contract for the able such place have executed and return both parts to me at your early convenience. The specification and copies of letters annexed there to which also be signed were marked in pencil. When the contract has been sealed by the Canal Company.

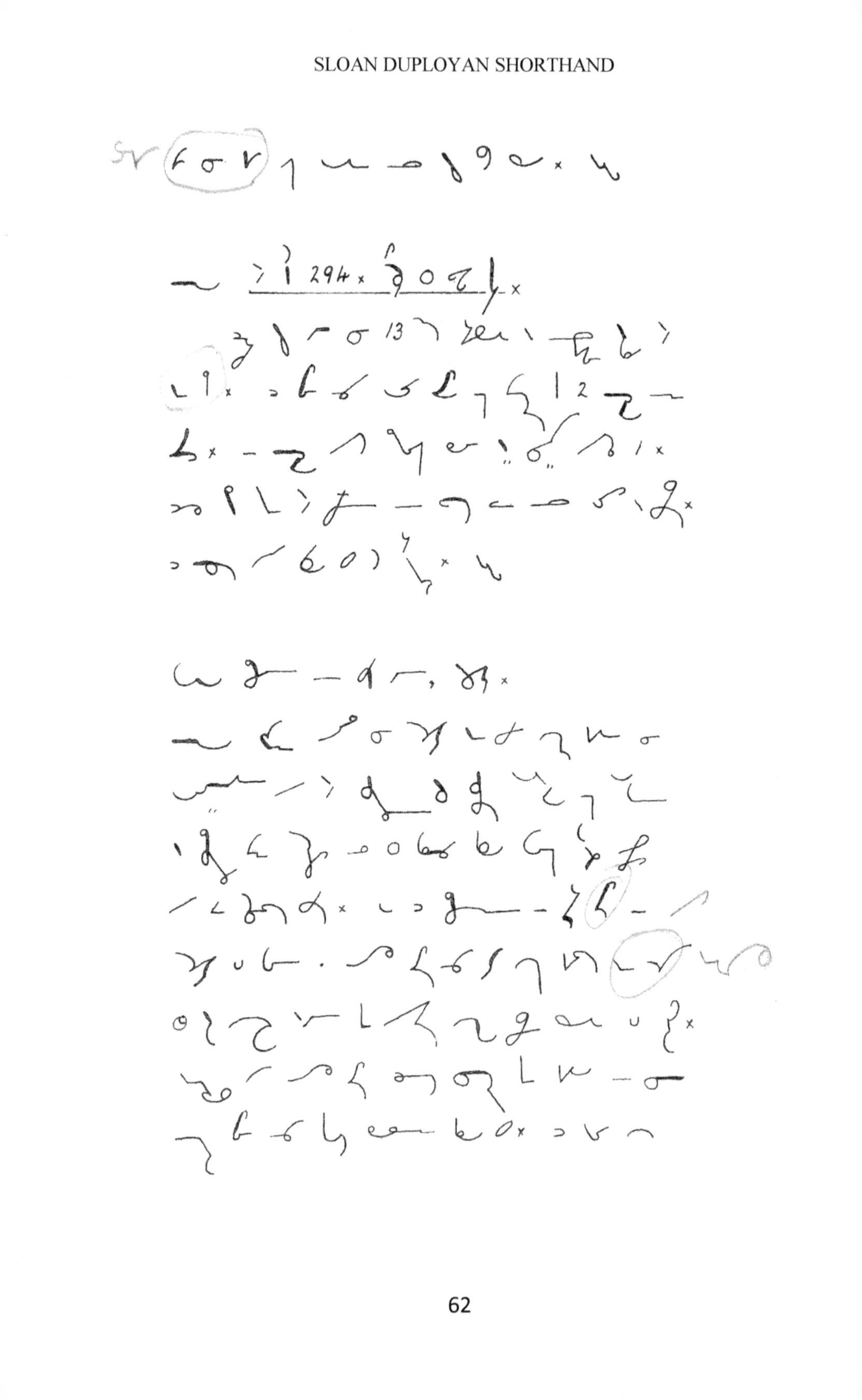

one of the parts will be sent to you for your own use. Yours faithfully.

Dear Sir Contract number 294. Reconstruction of railway bridge

We thank you for your letter of the 13th instant enclosing in duplicate formal contract for the able. We regret that our sale requires to be witnessed by 2 directors and the secretary. The directors are not available as the fair holds are now on. We shall however have the contract executed and return it to you early in August. We trust this will cause you no inconvenience. Yours faithfully.

M/s Arnold and cooper Ltd, Falkirk (city)UK.

Dear Sirs, With reference to the supply of the steel work for the coal shipping plant at Sunderland are contract provided from proposed sub contracts to be submitted for approval with the stipulation that all material possible was to be manufactured locally or on the north east coast. When we approached to an engineer regarding the steel work he made a special request that this work should be placed in the hands of a firm which was controlled by the largest shippers of coal, using his equipment. In the face of this special request. We had no alternative but to place the order and have much regret that this business has had to pass you. We feel sure

§ 16.

However, that you will understand the circumstances. Yours faithfully,

16.

M/s Black and Anderson Ltd, Gateshead (England)

Dear Sirs, further to our note of yesterday we have to state that we give our customer the information contained in your letter of even date. He informed, so that if delivery could be given in 4 weeks he would at once order from you 2 7' machines at a price of 210 pound each. After speaking to you on the telephone we informed him that we regretted that it was impossible to guarantee less than 6 weeks delivery. That you would do your best to intercept this but did not wish to mislead them. We through write a suggestion that you might be able to lend them a 5' gap machine. They said that this might solve the difficulty and we promised to make enquiry with you and let them know the position tomorrow. Yours faithfully.

M/s James Shaw and Co. Ltd, Carlisle (England)

Dear Sirs, we have your report of the 20th instant and note that you still have about 20 balls to draw over to complete the pairs. We see however, that

§ 17.

you soon to be getting on better with the cylinders and that you have started the concrete to and carrying at the north end. This leaves you a considerable amount of work to do if you hope to squeeze it in by the middle of October, the revised date for completion. We shall be glad if in your next report you will give us some indication of what position will be according to your estimate about the date referred to. It is possible that we may be able to make some excuse based on the abnormal bad weather but we wish you to review the whole position so that we may be fully informed. Yours faithfully

17.

The Duff town Dock Co. Ltd., Port Duff town (UK)

Dear Sirs, we have pleasure in enclosing herewith invoice in triplicate amounting to 6103 pound in respect of materials delivered to site in connection with the extension to the east side of Middle Dock. We shall be glad if you will grant a further interim certificate covering the period of work dispatched subsequent to 31 May last. We have received payments to the account amounting to 4000 pounds and we shall be glad to have a remittance for the balance due to us at your earliest convenience. Kindly note that the special bolts, nuts and washers are maintained priced at 26 pound per ton but this price will be adjusted in the final account. Our cash day

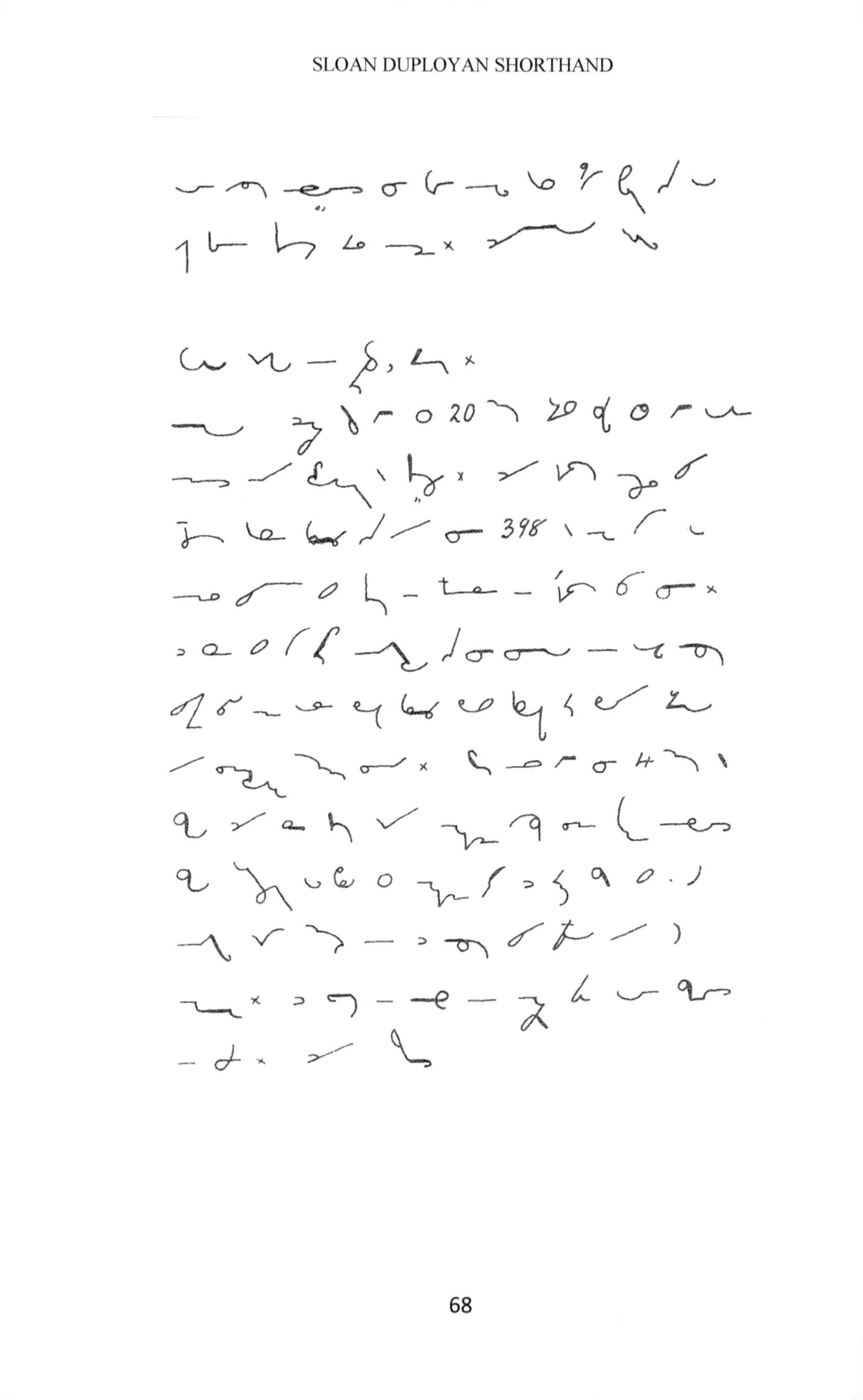

398

is the last Tuesday of the month and any sum of accounts you may have against us will be paid by cheque on that date. We are dear Sirs Yours Faithfully.

M/s Philips and Morgan, Cardiff (UK)

Dear Sirs, we thank you for your letter of 20th instant enclosed copy of a letter sent today to our representative in Bristol (city). We are pleased to note that you will dispatch some of the material against our order 398 in ten days' time and that you will do your best to expedite the completion of this order. We wrote to you yesterday regarding deliveries against other orders and sincerely trust that you will get along to the site as much material as you possibly can, as our erectors are, at the present time, standing idle. Referring to your letter of the 4th instant for hoppers we are rather praised in our template shop at the moment and as these hoppers involve any amount of template work we cannot offer you a quick delivery in this instance and we trust you will excuse our no tendering. We return the drawing and thank you for giving us the opportunity to quote. We are yours very truly.

§18.

18

M/s John Lawson Ltd, Burslehm (England)

Dear Sirs with reference to your letter of the 6th instant to our London office, we have pleasure in giving you our revised quotation for larger size riveting machine and trust that the same will meet your requirements. One patent scissors type hydraulic riveting machine having a gap of 7' 1/2" and a delight of 18" suitable for a working pressure of 1200 pound per square inch giving a load on rivet of 40 tons. Price 217 pound. We enclose print showing generally to machining quoted for. The extra price for an additional large operating valve will be 15 pound. The cast steel arms of these machines are of tough cast steel with forged steel pin and fitted with special hydraulic gun metal piston with easily replaceable letter packing between valve and cylinder operatering valve of the rotary face type, copper pipe connections also gun metal relief valve. The arms are fitted with special steel bolsters and die holders and special steel dies, one plane injure to suspend the machine with axis of dies at right angles to the suspension axis. We trust that this short description will give you a fair indication of the machine we are offering you. Trusting to hear of your final decision in the near future we are. Yours faithfully.

M/s Stapleton and Dense, Renfrew (Scottland).

Dear Sirs, with reference to my interview with you Mr Dense on the 5th instant I have pleasure in enclosing the draft of our proposed final account for this work. Referring to the last item for additional excavation, I think I have mentioned all my points in support of our claims at my interview. Briefly it is that our price was best on your drawing no. 254 and this excavation is additional to that drawing. I would be pleased to give any further particulars desired and which you wish I would be glad to appear before your Board and state our case for this claim. No doubt your directors will give the matter due consideration and as soon as a decision is reached, I shall be glad if you will advise me without delay. With reference to your enquiry of the 6th instant I have to state that the level and staff were handed over to Mr. Maxwell to enable him to carry out certain private work and he undertook table response for their safe return. I have taken up the matter with the people for whom he was acting and they state that they dispatched the level and staff and 2 tripods to Glasgow prepaisetering on the 2 April at the same time advising the consignee of dispatch. With regard to the typewriter this was the last item to leave and was sent to the head office on the 30 March as one piece of machinery and its despatch duly advised. I trust you will find upon enquiry that the various items have reached the proper destinations. Yours truly.

ℰ 19.

19.

M/s Edwards and Michael Bromwich (England)

Dear Sirs, In answer to your enquiry of yesterday regarding the prime amount factors of welding in a brakashion, the following are the features we would specify. All longitude joints and all circular joints must be subjected to x-ray examination to prove the soundness of the weld. All pressure vessels must be stress relieved after welding. These elements the tendency there and weakness and brittleness in welds nose trade and removes the danger of localised corrosion. The vessel those, goes into service without inherent stress. The bend test specified must be most rigid --- not less than 30 percent elongation of all outside fibres as compared with 20 percent for standard specifications. The tensile strength of the joint as shown by the test must be not less than 100 percent of that of the plate. The elongations of the weld metal itself must be not less than 20 percent in 2". The specification gravity must be not less than 7.80 assuring the prime absence of porosity. Some types of welding do not require a density determination. Qualification tests of welders should be made continuously during production through test plates. Should it be convenient for your representative to visit our works? We would be pleased to afford him facilities.

for observing all the forging tests. Yours faithfully

The Western Shipping Co., Cardiff (UK)

Dear Sirs, with regard to the adjustment of propulsion to be applied to your contemplated new paddle steamer, we would suggest 'Diesel' electric machinery. There are several advantages attached to this form of propulsion in the net. Least being in view of the purpose for which the boat is intended, a larger space for passenger accommodation then is possible with the older methods of propulsion. 4 8 cylinder 4 stroke 'Diesel' electric wans would develop 1300 sent I put ample for a vessel of the dimensions you state that a gross tonnage of 450. In the installation we have in mind the main propulsion motor would consider of 2 machines in tandem provided with special features for marine duty. 4 main generators would be provided for supplying power to the propulsion motors. Each would be of the self-ventilated type running at 600 revolutions per minute. An auxiliary generator would be coupled in tandem with each main generator. A new feature that would be worth considering would be the intent of a motor directly on the paddle shaft. If you are verbally disposed towards these addresses we shall be glad to submit drawings and specifications for your consideration. Yours faithfully.

¶ 20.

20.

I A Hamilton Esq, Canterbury (England)

Dear Sir, William Hamilton's Trust

Please refer to our meeting today; we enclose a note of the estate as at 31st December. The 2 bonds and dispositions in security amounting all together the 1800 pound cannot immediately for the reasons explained but realised. There is no difficulty in dividing among yourself and your stores the 500 pound 'First Safety Investment Co. Ltd.' Redeemable debenture and the 2290 pound of railway stocks the total of these on the account values as at 31st December being 2780 pounds are terrible. We could also of course realise the ground annuals amounting to 1300 pounds. On the other hand if the desire of your due stores is to give you into a certain income you could only divide the stocks we have previously referred to and could direct the trustees to pay you into the income in respect of the ground annuals and the bonds and disposition in security. The total of this income is about 140 pound, gross tax falling to be deducted. You cannot however, accept by special arrangements make this into your hands income as it would really be the income of yourself and stores. We trust this mix to make the position clear. We understand that it is your desire and that of your stores to make up to you into an income of 150 pound per annum. Your suggestion is that as regards to income

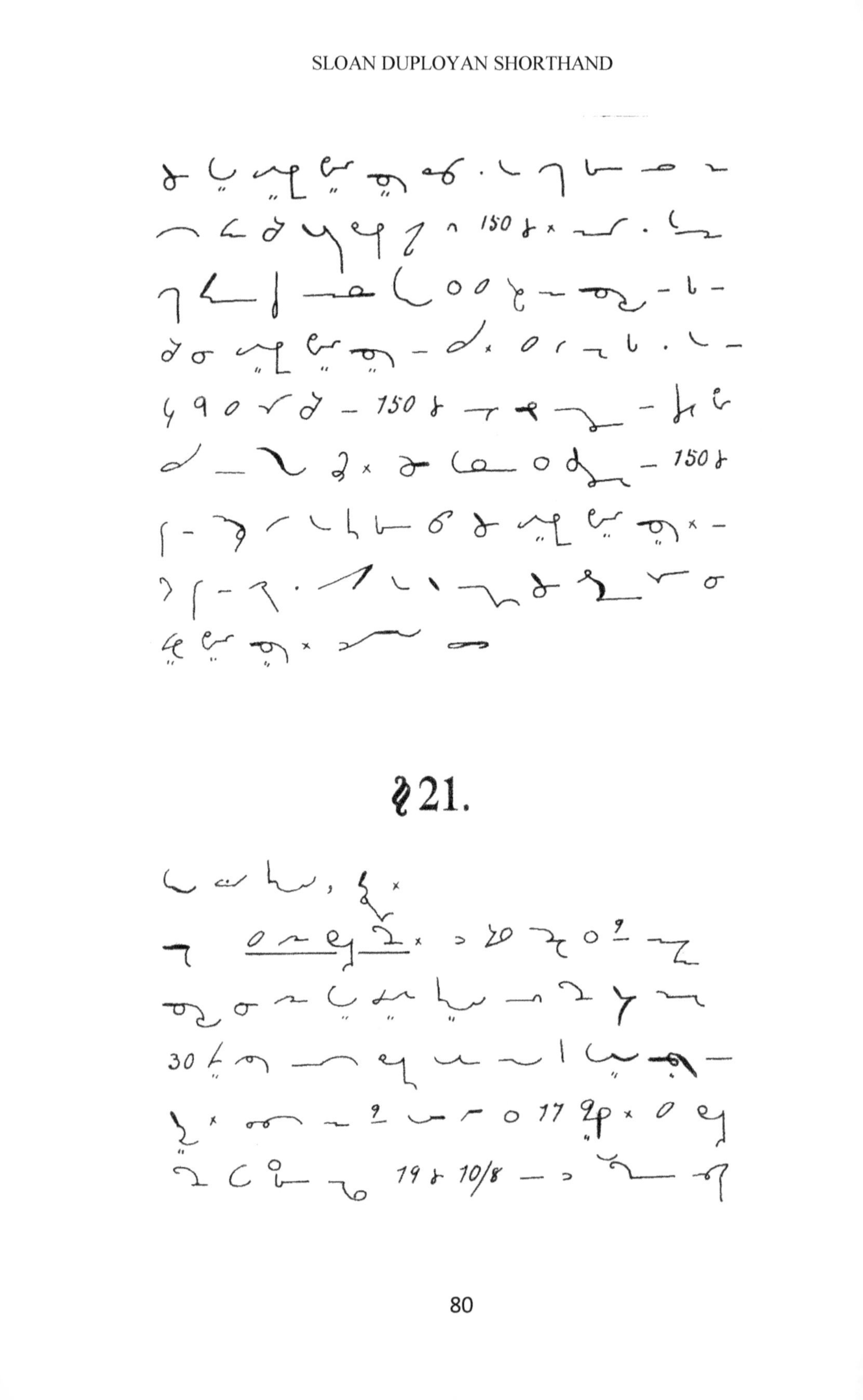

§ 21.

from the M/s Elsability Hamilton Trust right of this a sum should be paid to you into which with the income receivable as a bill will give him 150 pound. To do this, a mandate should be granted by you and to other members of your family to the trustees to pay the income of the Elsability Hamilton Trust to yourself. You would then pay a sum to make up your hand's income to 150 pounds and would thereafter divide the balance among yourself and stores equally. Another method of providing the 150 pound would be to instruct this sum being paid wholly from the Elsability Hamilton Trust. The effect would be to leave a larger sum for division from the life earned fund of the William Hamilton Trust. We are, Dear Sir Yours truly.

21

M/s Ethel Benson, Caernarfon (UK)

Dear Mr. your late Hosbense Estate. We enclose statement of account to do with the trustees of the late Ms Katling Benson and her Estate for the year ending 30th June last and which has been sent to us by M/s Driver and Furness. Attached to the account is their letter of 17th October. Your Hosbense Estate was over paid the sum of 19 pound 10/8 and we suggested that this would be

19 8 10/8

0 29

adjusted between yourself and your children but you will see in their letter attached to the account that they would prefer that the money be repaid to the Estate. The matter is rather complicated and we have not really taken the trouble to peruse the account carefully and go right into it. Probably you and your sons will understand the position without any clause enquiry on our part and we shall be glad, therefore, if you will deal with the matter and return the account to us together with M/s Driver and Furness's letter and let us view cheque for 19 pound 10/8 to send on if you agree to repay the money. If you wish us to go fully into the matter and understand it thoroughly and advise you we shall of course be prepared to do so but we should have to charge a considerable fee for the answer. We are dear madam yours faithfully

See the Loose Esq, Etenbro (Edinburgh)

Dear Sir, Bernard Johnson's Trust.

We duly received your letter of 29 ult. (ultimo) asking for a certificate of deduction on income tax from income from the able Trust payable to you and others M/s Jaint Deeves for the year ending 5th April. We are afraid, however, that we cannot grant a certificate of tax deducted from the payments made to you and others, as although the income is paid to her under authority given to us by you for income tax purposes the income really belongs to you.

§ 22.

The mandate authorizing us to pay to you and others during her lifetime so revocable at any time and the position is that the income is gifted to her each half year as during paid to him. We however, enclose a certificate of deduction of tax from your share of the income which should be shown in your income tax return or claim. We are, Dear Sirs, Yours truly.

22.

Lenard Thachure Esquire, Leeds

Dear Sir. Yourself have buller. In accordance with the instructions given to us on the 28th ult. we wrote to the Great Rex insurance co. ltd. to present your claim for compensation. We have now received a reply from the company. A copy of which, we are enclosing herewith. You will see from the letter that a representative of the company called here and we were able to arrange the terms which we think you will consider satisfactory. We also enclose the form of discharge which you might sign across the stamp and return to us when we shall settle with the company. In regards to the question of expenses we stated to the company that if they admitted liability before the end of last week we should waive the question of expenses. We propose to charge you a fee of 2 genies. Yours faithfully

M/s Bent and Burnet, Leeds (UK)

Dear Sirs, Thachure Vee Buller. We hereby acknowledge the receipt of your communication of the 28th ult. and we confirm our representative's visit and conversation with you Mr Burnet. We also confirm that we are prepared to meet your client without, however, any admission of liability to the extent of 20 genes in payment of his claim for damages suffered through the accident on 22 July last. Enclosed is a discharge form and we shall be obliged if you will kindly have this signed by your client and returned to us when we shall issue the necessary cheque. As you arranged with our representative the question of legal expenses does not arise in consideration of our making a prompt offer to settle the claim. We await your reply. Yours faithfully

Thomas Baldwin Esquire, Mayfield (Village in England)

Dear Sir, regarding the jolly firms. In this matter, case before the Court, this afternoon the Chairman of the licensing bench declined to hear the application stating that at the time the Bear and Wine license was renewed it was understood that the question of the music license was to stand over until the renewal day in January when it would be dealt with. This statement Mr. Bromley declined to admit but of course there was no controlling the Court and the

Application was accordingly withdrawn and it will have to remain over until January to see what line the bench will take then. Yours truly

M/s Yong and Right Cliff, Dublin (City in Ireland)

Dear Sirs 25 St. Johns Road. I am in receipt of your letter of even number dated….. with enclosure and note appointment to complete tomorrow at 10-30. I send you here with an apportionment account. The last receipt for payment of rent charge will be provided to you on completion. Yours faithfully

Alexander Metcalf Esq, Glasgow (UK)

Dear Sir, Estate of the late Thomas Morging

The security we have for 1400 pounds is 10 dwelling houses being numbers 6 to 24 on the western side of Albert Street each house being let at 7 shilling per week on our paying taxes. They have been valued by M/s Wilkinson's and Mills of 91 Victoria Road at 2000 pound and they consider it a good trusty security for 1400 pound. We shall be glad to know whether the trustees could see their way to entertain the security deficits shall be obliged by your letting

¶23.

us have cheque for 1400 pound as soon as possible. Your truly

23.

M/s Don and Pomfret, Salisbury (UK)

Dear Sirs, Johns the Fuller

I return the draft conveyance perused and approved as altered in red. I enclose the policy as requested which is in the names of the vendors and his/their mortgagees. The vendor is willing that the policy should be endorsed in the name of the client by the mortgagee may prefer to wait until completion. In that event my client has no objection to hold the policy in trust for your client until completion. Yours truly

M/s Roberts and Street, Barmouth (UK)

Dear Sirs, Andson and Co. and Barkley.

Referring to our Mr. Bliss interview with you Mr Roberts on Saturday last he has as suggested some Mr. Marks with a view to obtaining the well source consent to M/s Barkley Time, the house to our clients. Mr. Marks will not however, for one moment entertain to hardly but he now informs us that he is prepared to advise his client for a consideration to give

him consent to the assignment of the lease right and at the M/s Anson and Co. He further informs us that his client will be in St. Alliance in the course of the next 2 or 3 year and he will communicate with us in due course after seeing him. Yours truly

M/s Williams and Bothomley Market, Draethen (UK).

Dear Sirs, We are instructed by M/s Smith and Co. to apply to you for payment of the sum of 18 pounds being the amount of account rendered by them to you for goods sold and delivered. Unless this amount together with 3/7 or charges be paid to us by noon on **Wednesday** next. We shall proceed against you for the recovery thereof without further notice. Yours truly.

Hasakt Williams Esquire, Leeds

Dear Sir, Estate of the late Jain Guns

We have prepared a draft deed of family arrangement making you a trusty jointly with Ms Williams and we enclosed it for your perusal. The skilled and trained schedules refer to in the draft are necessarily incomplete. Until it has been agree upon those claims

§24.

paid we are not in a position to complete them. We shall be obliged if you will kindly carefully peruse the draft and let us have your views in regard there to. You will notice that we have answered provisions enabling the trustees to resort to the capital and we shall like to know what amount should be limited in any one year to be drawn there at; also that in the event of Ms Williams being married a sum of money should be payable right of the capital to her. Her share in the carpus being debited there with. The only matter that we have not dealt with in the draft is the question of furniture purchased by M/s Williams at the sale. So this to be treated as a debt against her fare if this head of to be provided for in the draft, or as assets of the trust? If so it can then be dealt with in the third schedule of the decd. Will you kindly mention to Ms. Williams that she has not sent us the accounts referred to in our last letter and in respect of which we wrote. Yours truly.

24.

Alexander Mitchel Esq, Dundee (UK).

Dear Sir, We thank you for your letter of yesterday returning signed the minutes which we have sent you on the 14th inst. When we prepared the minutes we understood that Major Endersons and Mr. Finlesons had in fact resigned so that on receipt of

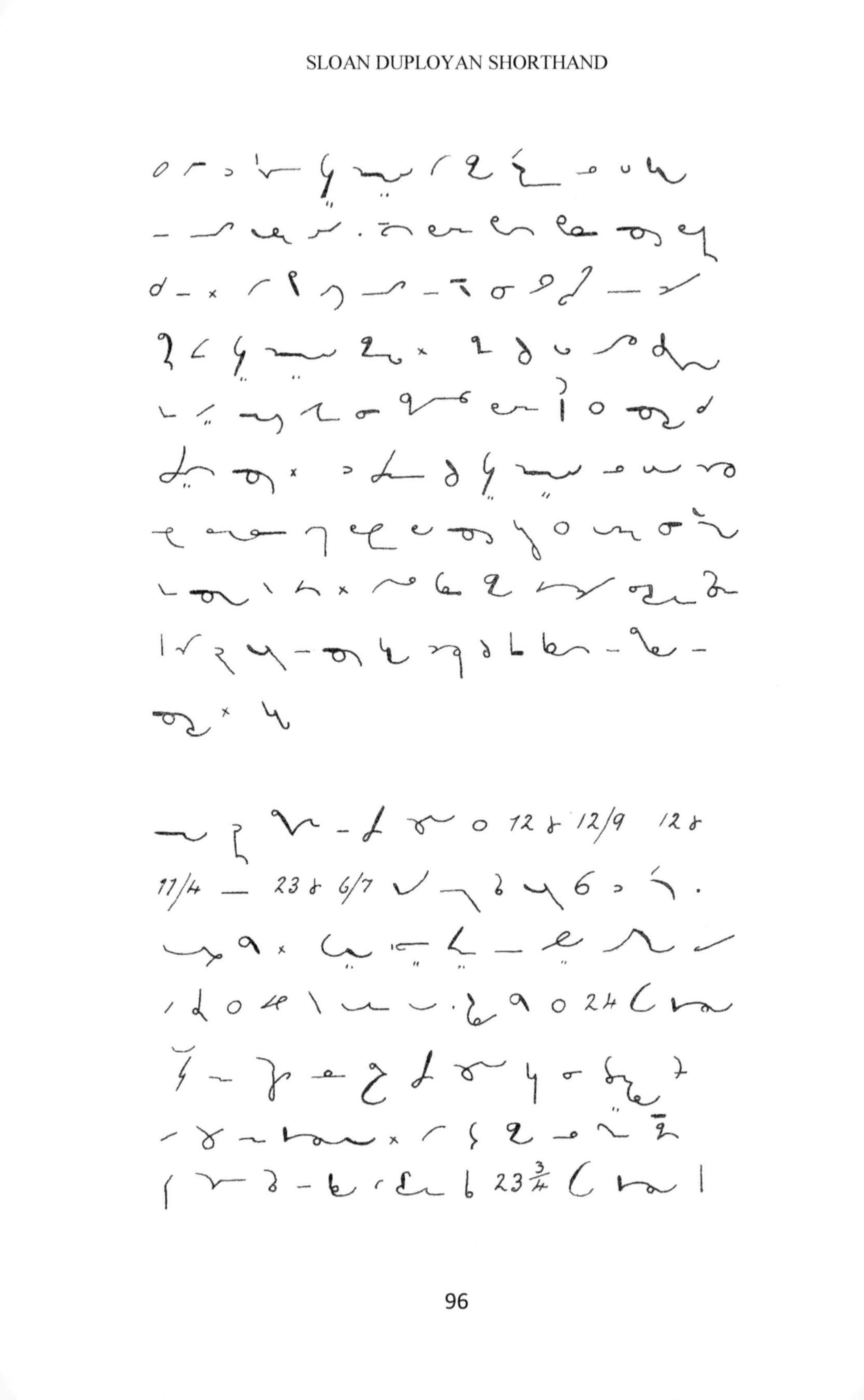

your letter we telephoned Major Anderson who of course confirmed that he prefers the delay in signing until a decision as to the assumption of some other trusty has been come to. This however, will not delay the transfer of the law agency and we are arranging with Major Andersons accordingly. Apart from any special provisions in the Will there is no limit **either** up or down as to the number of trustees on a quotation trust. We gathered from Major Anderson that he is anxious that some right side should be assumed as trustee in view of certain other interests in the trusts in question. This is a matter of course in which we are at present **ignorant** but once we have received the trust papers we shall be in a better position to advise the trustees. Yours faithfully

Dear Sir, We have been advertising the ground annuals of 12 pound 12/9 12 pound 11/4 and 23 pound 6/7 for self and have now received what we consider a satisfactory offer. M/s Read Grant and Luis superstores here on behalf of clients have sent us a formal offer of 24 years purchase subject to the stipulation that the a full year's ground annuals payable at Martenmise next will fall to the purchasers. This means of course that if the transaction could be settled now the price would represent about 23 ¾ years purchase but

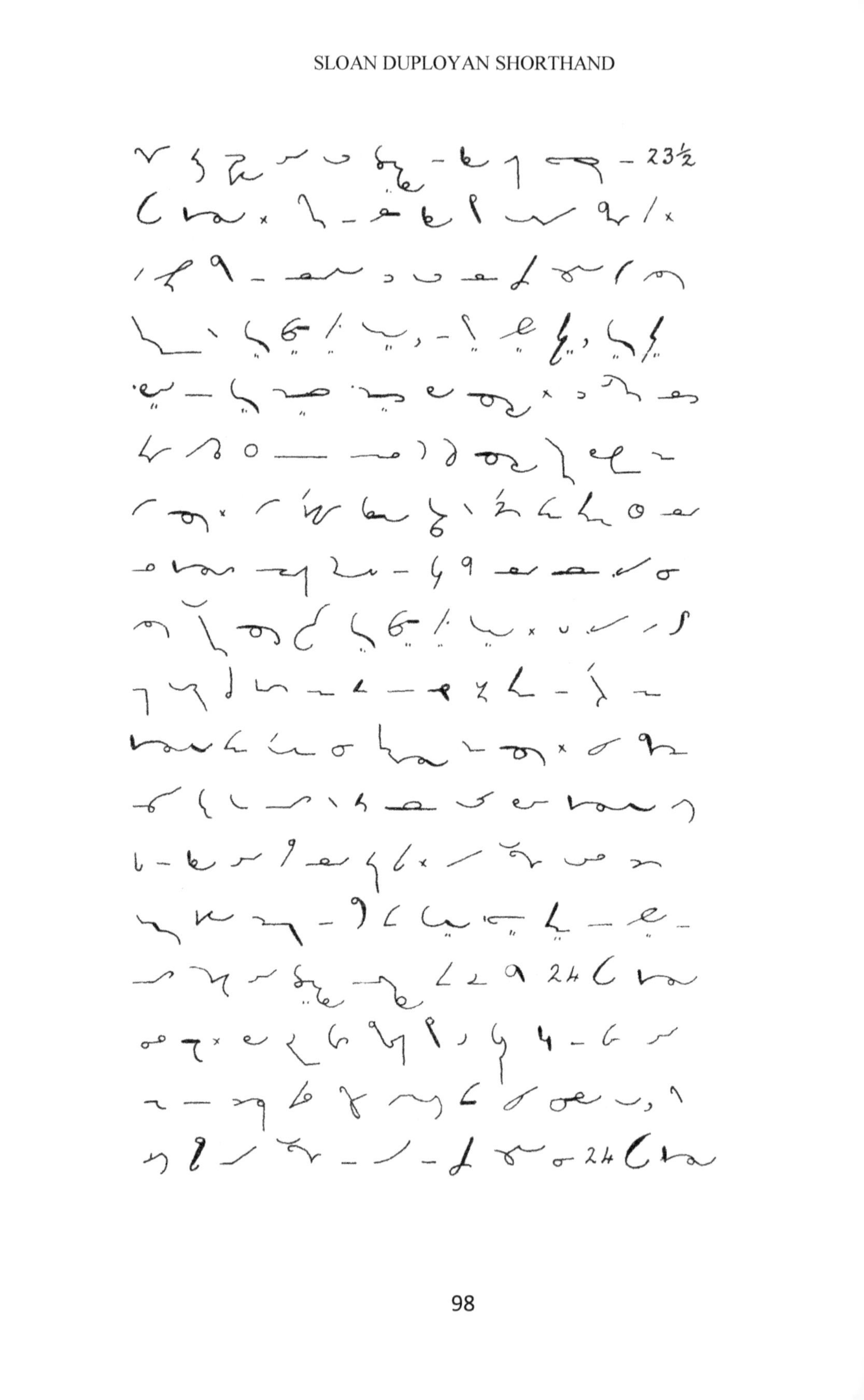

if this cannot take place until see Mortenmise the price will be reduced to 23 ½ years purchase. Even the lighter price however, is in our opinion good. On looking over the titles we see that the ground annuals were last visited in by Mr Wolter J Sons, the Reve Loyee Gregory, Mr. Gorge Harson and Mr. Andrew Handry as trustees. We understand that these gentlemen are now all did and that no new trustees have been assumed into this trust. This complicates matters somewhat in connection with the granting of a title that purchaser and it will be necessary to make up the title through the heir of the last surviving trusty who was Mr. Wolter J Sons. His heir will require to be served by a petition to the Court and thereafter erecting grant to convince to the purchasers with the consent of the beneficiaries in the trust. You will appreciate that this will mean some delay in carrying through the sale as the purchasers will not pay the price until a good title can be given. Our suggestion is that we should in the first place endeavour to arrange with M/s Reed Grant and Luees to delay settlement until Martinmise and if possible get them to offer 24 years purchase at a term. As they have the money available however they may not be prepared to wait until then and we shall be glad if you will let us know whether you will authorise us, if they will not agree to our suggestion to circulate the ground annuls at 24 years purchase

§25.

allowance their clients to collect the whole a full year's ground annuals at Mortinmise in such a case we should stipulate that the price will be placed now on deposit receipt in joint names and the trust will go to the benefit of the deposit receipt interest. We may of course be able to arrange a compromise between these 2 suggested prices. Yours faithfully.

25.

D. L. Mackenzie Esq., Nork (London)

Dear Sir,   The trust account

We have now received from Mr. Geferis the trust accounts which we have sent to him and are in a position to deal with the various matters raised by you in your last 2 letters. The utilisation of part of the capital funds of a trust to meet annual right against depends on the experience that the parties interested in the Trust Estate should each bear the expenses appropriate to their interest; those though entitled to the revenue of the trust pre write off that revenue the expenses incidental to its collection, the normal repair work required on the irritable property and the law agents and auditors fees so for as applicable to the management of and accounting for income. The beneficiaries ultimately entitled to the capital of the Estate are the trust, on the other hand, are charged with the expenses incidental

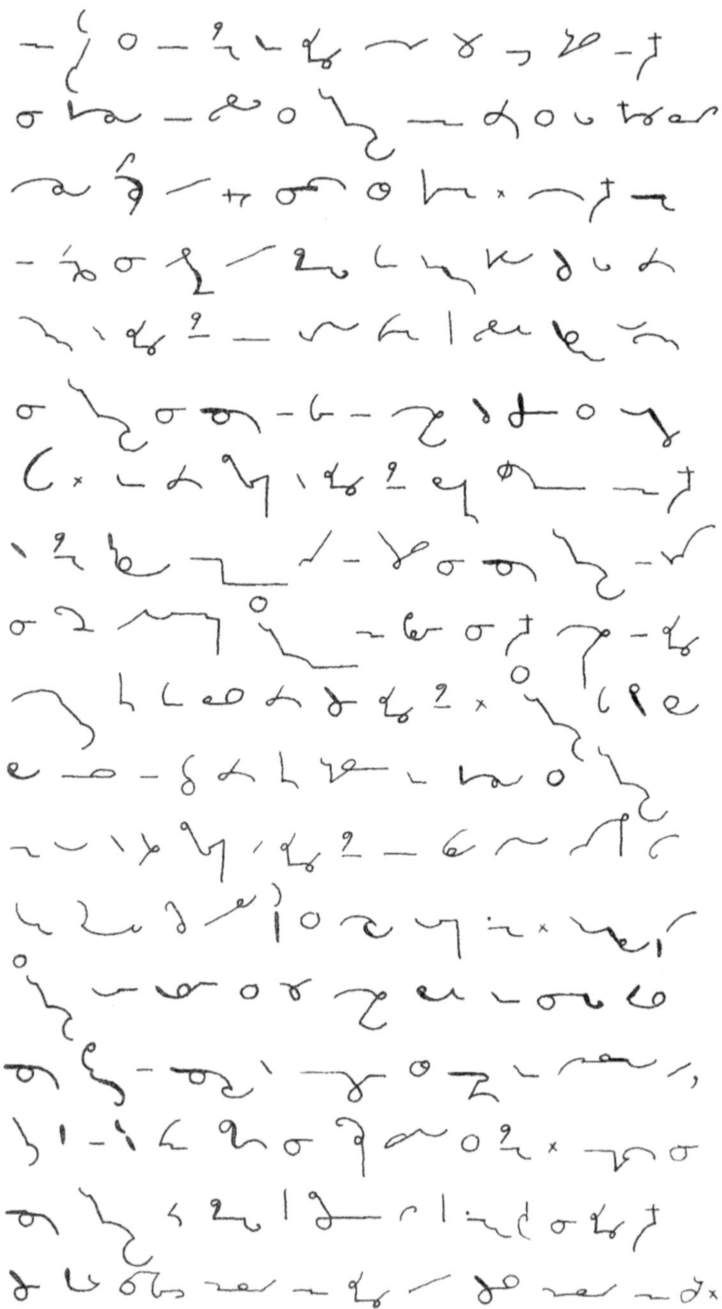

B.L.   E

to the management of and accounting for the capital which will fall to them includes the expenses of the purchase and realisation of investments and the cost of any exceptional right ly such as reconstruction or extension alteration of a building. Such expenses during the continuance of the life rent are accordingly met in the first place from any cash standing in capital account and when this is one thing be realising from time to time suggestion of the investments of the trust to meet the charges for a period of several years. End cash available in the capital account has been exhausted and the expenses for accounting purposes debited against the value of the trust investments. The funds of the estate are said to be over invested to the amount of the expenses chargeable to capital which have not been met to write off cash from the capital account. Over investment may however, also arise due to more cash being employed in the purchase of investments Ten is in fact available on capital account and while this is undesirable way some time necessary if a royal number of shares is to be obtained. In so for as per this over investment is the result of annual charges arising in the ordinary course of trust administration the trustees in default of a direction in the distatures will have no power to interfere with the operation of the stable rules of accounting. Depletion of the trust investments can accordingly be avoided only by obtaining payment of the capital expenses from the persons ultimately entitled to the capital are from those entitled to the income.

26 & 5 — 16 & 16

The lighter course would not state the giving of instructions to the trustees by all the persons entitled to the income of each trust that all expenses were to be paid write off income. If it is impossible to obtain the consent of all of the life renters to this course. It would be possible to charge the expenses on the shares all income falling to talk and consent by this would be manifestly unfair. We annex a note of the annual expenses and of the cash balances in the capital account in each of the Morison Trust and the Garden Trust as shown in the last 2 accounts and in a cash statement supplied to us by M/s Dean and O'connor. We have not included the details of the charges in the trust investment which also affect the position. The figure brought out in the cash statement in such a case is subject that deduction in respect of proportion of M/s Dean and O'connors accounts chargeable to income, the whole amount of these accounts chargeable since the last trust account having been debited without allocation being capital and revenue. It will however, in the ordinary course by necessary to debit capital in each trust with a proportion of the auditor's fees of 26 pound 5 shillings and 16 pound 16 shillings respectively now outstanding. In the case of the Henderson Trust cash was available in capital account as a result of a change in the investments during the year

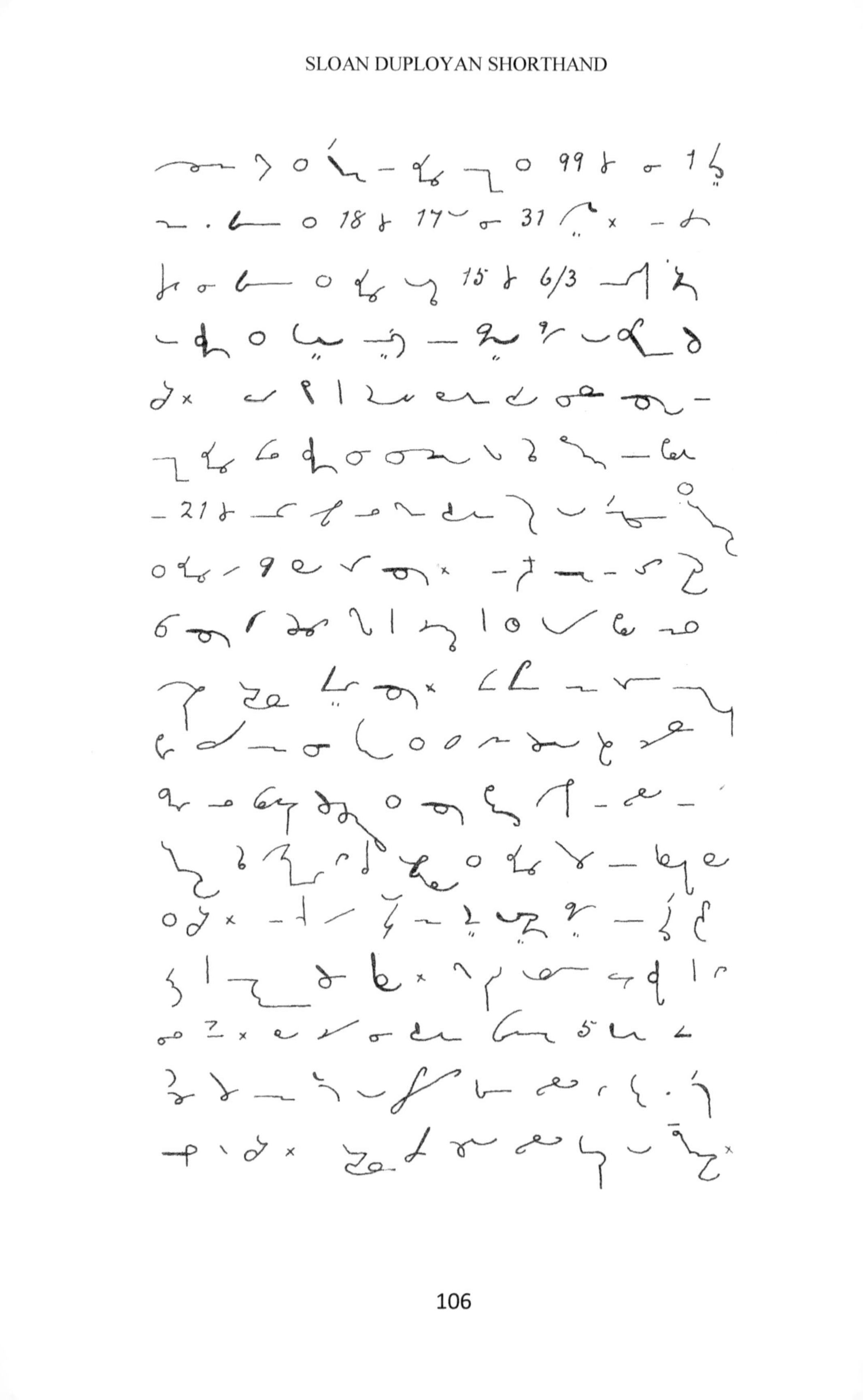

which had the effect of converting the capital debt of 99 pound at 1st January into a credit of 18 pound 17 shillings at 31st December. The cash balance at credit of capital is now 15 pound 6/3 dollar will be increased in the proportion of M/s Dean and Occuner's account so recovered from income. It will however be necessary as in the case of the other trusts to debit capital without proportion of the auditors fee now outstanding and amounting to 21 pound and it is likely that if the present system is continued over investment of capital will occur also in this trust. The expenses during the early stages of this trust were naturally heavy but they should now be of a similar amount to those chargeable in the case of the Garden Trust. With regard to the fund divisible among yourself and the other members of your late father's family. We are of the opinion that while it would be from the point of view of Trust administration desirable to realise the investments now this can be done only by a sacrifice of capital value and possibly also of income. The bonds are subject to the Rent Restriction Acts and consequently repayment cannot be demanded from the borrowers. If they could be sold, it would probably be only at a discount. As they are at present yielding 5 percent on their nominal value and the interest is regularly paid realisation would mean a considerable drop in income. In the case of the ground annuals realisation might not be so disadvantageous.

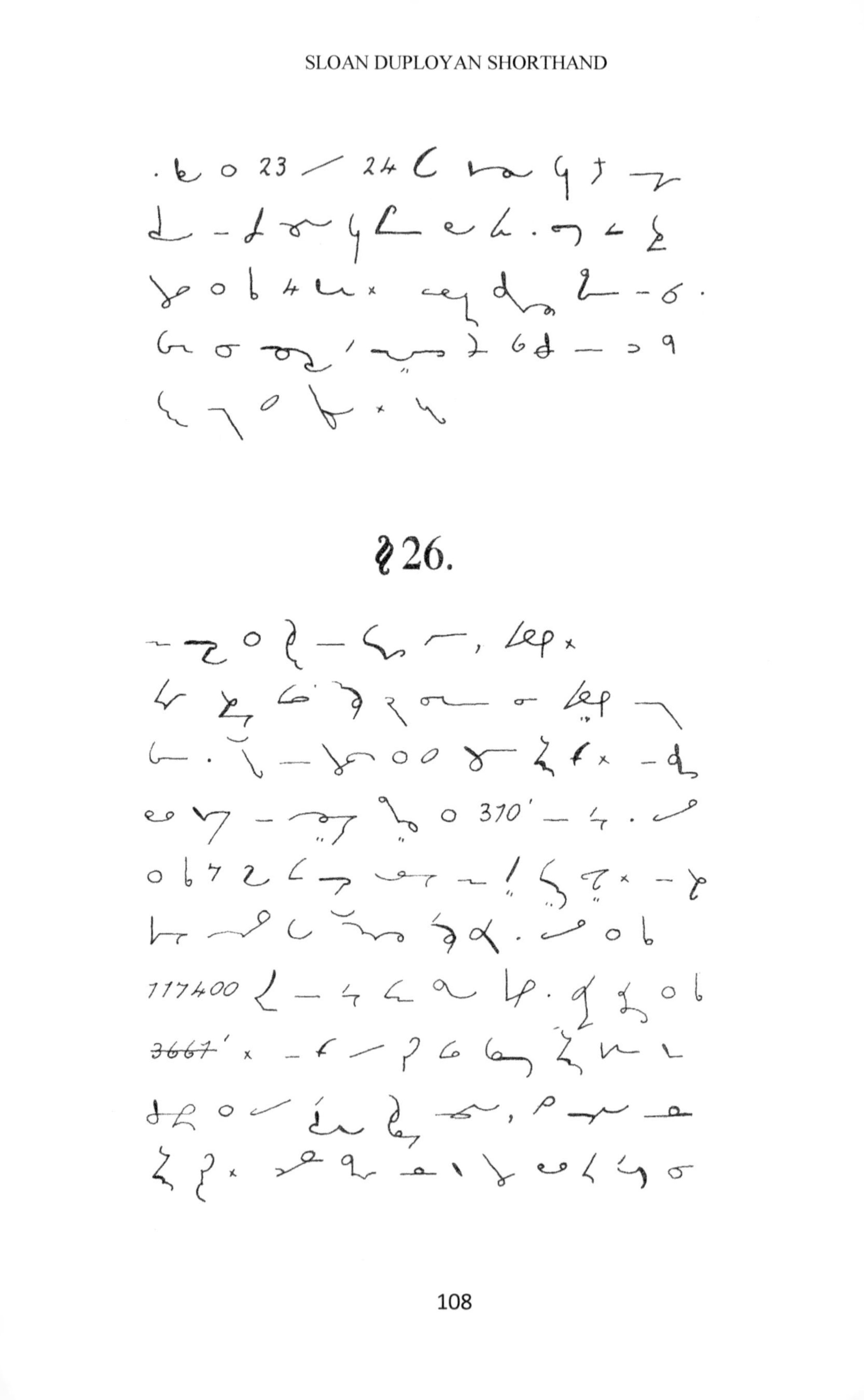

§ 26.

A price of 23 or 24 years purchase may be expected and on this basis the ground annual may be regarded as giving a return on their market value of about 4 percent. It has been provisionally agreed to hold a meeting of the trustees on Thursday next 6 approx and we hope to maintain to have your views. Yours faithfully.

26.

To the Directors of Newmen and Westernly Ltd., Glossop (UK).

Gentlemen, in accordance with your instructions, we have attended at Glossop and have made a subway and violation of you, for old engineering works. The property has a front good the Chadwick Avenue of 310' and contains an area of about 7 acres with a direct side hence to the Grey Western Railway. The factory buildings which are of most substantial construction cover an area of about 1117400 square feet and contain with the office block a cubical capacity of about 3661000 feet. The works are equipped with a modern engineering plant for the production of air compressors, pneumatic tools, lower drills and other engineering equipment. We are of the opinion that the fair value as a going concerned of the

§ 27.

I have been mentioned for old engineering works together with the fixed and loose plant and machinery and effects therein as at 30th September was the sum of 154232 pound and that would be a fair and proper figure to insert in your balance sheet as representing the value of those Assets. These figures are exclusive of the gages, and have gages and special tools, stock, stars, work in progress, patterns, drawings, patents and goodwill. We have also made a subway of the far old residences Brewmail Cardonald Road and 17 Wakefield Avenue which we value at 3000 pound making a total of 157232 pound. We are gentlemen, Yours faithfully.

27.

A F Topples Esq., London West

Dear Sir, We have made a careful inspection of the 4 properties referred to in your letter of 25th ult. (of last month) with a view to advising your asset the fair value of the same to the trust. We have obtained figures of income and write against which show that the properties are held on the following terms: Bank House Queen Street, lease 85 years ground rent 2000 pound; 18-24 Belmont Street lease 97

¶ 28.

years ground rent 1200 pound 151-159 Victoria Street lease 78 years ground rent 4400 pound 45-46 Governor Road lease 31 years ground rent 335 pound. With the exception of the building none has 45-46 Governor Road these properties are of recent construction and indeed with every modern conveyance. Numbers 45-46 Governor Road is an older building but has been thoroughly well maintained and is in substantial condition. We are informed that in respect of each property a mortgage has been effected and that such mortgages cannot be called in saloon assets and due instalments of capital and interest are paid. The annual rate of interest being in 2 cases 5 percent and in 2 cases 6 percent. We have given the matter our careful consideration and having regard to the class and situation of the properties and to the terms of the mortgages we are of the opinion that the value of these secrets to the trust is the sum of 412573 pound. Yours faithfully.

28.

M/s Priestley Henderson's and Co., Carlisle (UK)

Dear Sirs, In terms of your instructions of 7th inst. I have carefully examined the

properties 31-43 Hill view Thries. The property comprises a tenement of 3 storeys flat at front; in addition there is a back saloon and under the hall an extensive basement. The front building has an average length of about 67 feet and a width of 38'9". The back court for the tenement is formed by the flat roof of saloons connected with shops and is therefore at the first floor level. The court is right narrow, being only 13' in width except at the south end where the width is 17' for a distance of 12'. The back boundary is formed by a lane and between the lane and the back buildings there is a small piece of vacant ground. The Background at lane is on a level with basement floor. The front wall of tenement able shops is faced with a head for eastern assurer, simple in design by having 2 columns of aerials. The back wall adble court level is built of Red Roble mesurmation. The basement and saloon form a projection at back 2 storeys in at, the exterior wall being built of break sub fest with roof cast. The flat roof or court at projection is covered with asphalt and the roof of the front building is covered with slates. The adjoining tenements have enclosed front plots but asset tenement under description has shops, the width of plots is formed as an inter footpath. There is rather footpath which is the normal footpath along the

13' 9"

15'

31

33, 35, 39, — 41

43

334 13/8

37 14/7

terrace. The accommodation is as follows: Basement extending from under the inner footpath the back line of the building by expecting a small part 13'9" by 15' at the north corner is occupied as a bill yard room with 7 full sized tables and one small table. There is within the premises a small office store and lavatory accommodation. The bill yard room access in front at number 31 is by a stair in the front plot of the tenement to the south and I assume, as this is a permanent stair in use that the title provides for the right of access; there is also a back door to the lane. Numbers 33, 35, 39 and 41 are single shops of various sizes with back saloons. Number 43 was constructed for a shop but has been made into a house of 2 apartments. First floor has 3 flats of 2 rooms and a kitchen with a bedroom and hot and cold water. Second floor has the same arrangements. 3 doors on a lending is rather unusual for this class of house. The property is in fair order and is wholly occupied. The sanitary accommodation is ample and would meet the contemplated requirements of the present Housing Bill in Parliament. The shop rents are moderate but no increase could be expected during the period and conditions. The total rental amounts to 334 pound 13/8 and the annual ground burdens are stated at 31 pound 14/7. I value the property at the sum of

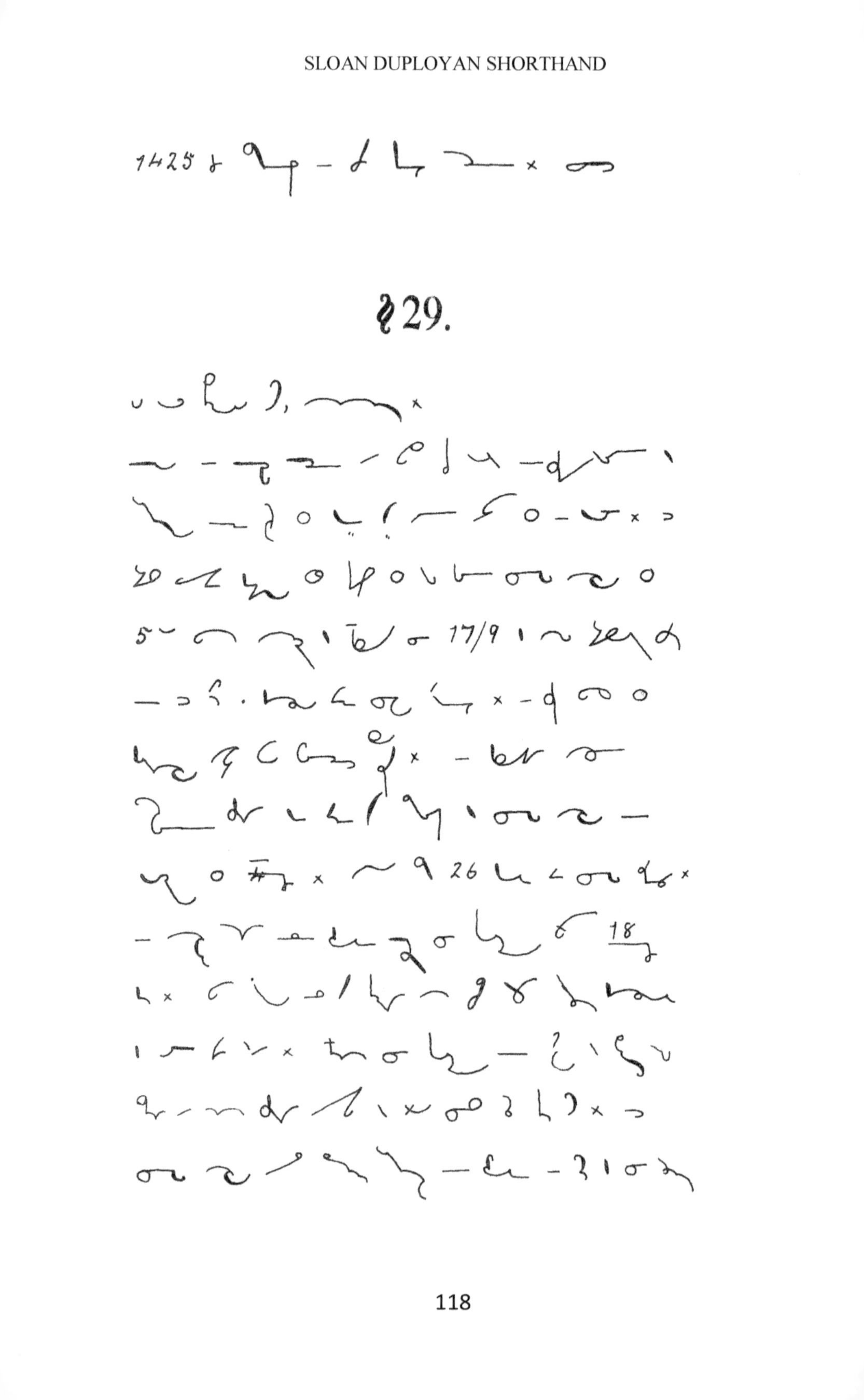

¶29.

1425 pound over and above the ground burdens stated. Yours Truly

29.

A C Robinson Esq, Chichester (UK)

Dear Sir the drapery trade will always be a safe and popular field for investors and the name of 'Smart Wear Ltd. Leeds' of the receipt. We enclosed herewith particulars of a block of fully paid ordinary shares of 5 shilling each which we have for disposal at 17/9 (17 shilling 9 pence) per share inclusive cost and we recommend a purchase with the utmost confidence. The public issue of preference shares this week was immediately oversubscribed. The prospects showed estimated profits for the current year available for ordinary shares and service of 400000 pound. This is offered 26 percent on the ordinary capital. The chairman states that the present turnover of the businesses exceeds 18000000 pound per annum. It is obvious that great benefits should accrue from this invoiced purchasing power under one control. Expansion of the business and economies in administration in his opinion will ensure profits largely in excess of those now being earned. These ordinary shares are an outstanding investment and represent the earning power of the financed

group of business at the top of the trade. You may safely purchase these shares as a sound permanent investment and with every confidence of improving the device. There has seldom being a finer combination put before investors. Every director is a respected name in the drapery trade and the management of the various undertakings is of first class order. If you will kindly sign and return the application form at foot along with your cheque, you can rely upon us then our items to supply the numbers you require. Yours faithfully

William and Michel Esquire, Tilbury (UK)

Dear Sir, We have pleasure in enclosing a copy of the proceedings at the recent annual meeting of Cast Stone Productions Ltd. As a shareholder in the company it will interest you to read it through. It will show you clearly the important progress that is already being made and we think you will agree that the future prospects are most encouraging. In spite of the improvement in the company's prospects the shares today can be obtained on more variable terms than ever before. We picked up a cheap lot yesterday from a man requiring immediate cash which we can offer at the moment at ½ per share free of commission as set out at foot. They are fully paid ordinary shares of 2 shilling each so far buying at this price, you will be purchasing at almost

⸮ 30.

half their face value. The man who puts a few of these away at the bottom of the box as a fair chance of doubling his capital before this year is right. On the other hand we have several increases for the shares at a slightly cheaper price so if you wish to dispose of your shares we would like to hear from you but it must not be taken that we recommend this course. Yours faithfully.

30.

Dear Sir, we have been approached by several other largest shareholders of 'Fillchair Harn Ltd. and Fillchair Harn Scotland Ltd. suggesting a merger of the 2 companies. The matter has been before us at several board meetings recently and has received our most careful attention and we have caught the conclusion that such a merger on the bases set out overleaf would be greatly to the interest of the shareholders. We have been limited to this conclusion by the following considerations

(1) speaking as a whole the present economic conditions throughout the year will call for every possible consolidation of resources by industrial companies. The universal reduction in purchasing power both at Home and abroad has check to demand for our goods, in consequence of such every avenue towards reduced overhead charges and will send cost of production must be explored to enable us to maintain our position in the highly

competitive markets of today.

(2) In particular the effect of the present adverse monetary conditions could be considerably off set, as the administration of the companies would under such an amalgamation be centralised and whereas at present time the sales Organisation of each company functions separately all though their foreign markets are often in close geographical proximity to proposed amalgamation would completely eliminated of which overlapping and hence enable administrative and operative charges to be reduced that considerable and greatly.

(3) Under the scheme the assets of both companies would be consolidated and the total share capital reduced by 50 percent. The effect being that I do have an earning stage would be reached sooner then on the present somewhat large capitalisation and also the shares themselves would consequently have a much higher market value. In order to give effect to the scheme of amalgamation it will be necessary for the shareholders of Fillchair Harn Scotland Ltd to agree that reduction of 50 percent other shareholding and the shares subsequently released will then be reissued to the shareholders of Fillchair Harn Ltd on the basis that (a) one 8 percent Preference share of 10 shilling each in Fillchair Harn Ltd will be exchanged for 5 shares of 2 shilling in Fillchair Harn Scotland Ltd. (b) 2 ordinary shares of 1 shilling each in Fillchair Harn Scotland Ltd will be exchanged for one share of 2 shilling each in Fillchair Harn Scotland Ltd. If the merger is carried through told out Assets of Fillchair Harn Ltd.

§ 31.

Include patents, trademarks rights, for old property, stock, debtors etc. will be automatically transferred to and become the property of Fillchair Harn Scotland Ltd. We have carefully considered the proposal put before us and have decided to recommend their acceptance. If you approve the scheme, kindly sign the enclosed card and return to the registered offices of the company as soon as possible and not later than 24 **June**. Yours faithfully.

31.

Dear Sir, The National Tea Stores Ltd.

We have pleasure in enclosing an offer for sale of fully paid ordinary shares of 5 shilling each at 25 shilling per share. This company's Preference Shares have always enjoyed. I can demand bills so the first opportunity given to investors to take an interest in the ordinary shares. Without a doubt the lists will be quickly closed. This company controls 415 shops, 2 factories and bakeries and 5 warehouses and those constitutes one of the most complete organisations in the country for manufacture and sale of essential food and stuff. The balance sheet disclosed in the offer for sale shows reserves and carry forward of more than a million pounds while list the good growth in the value of the company's properties many of which were asked before the war/year, constitutes a large

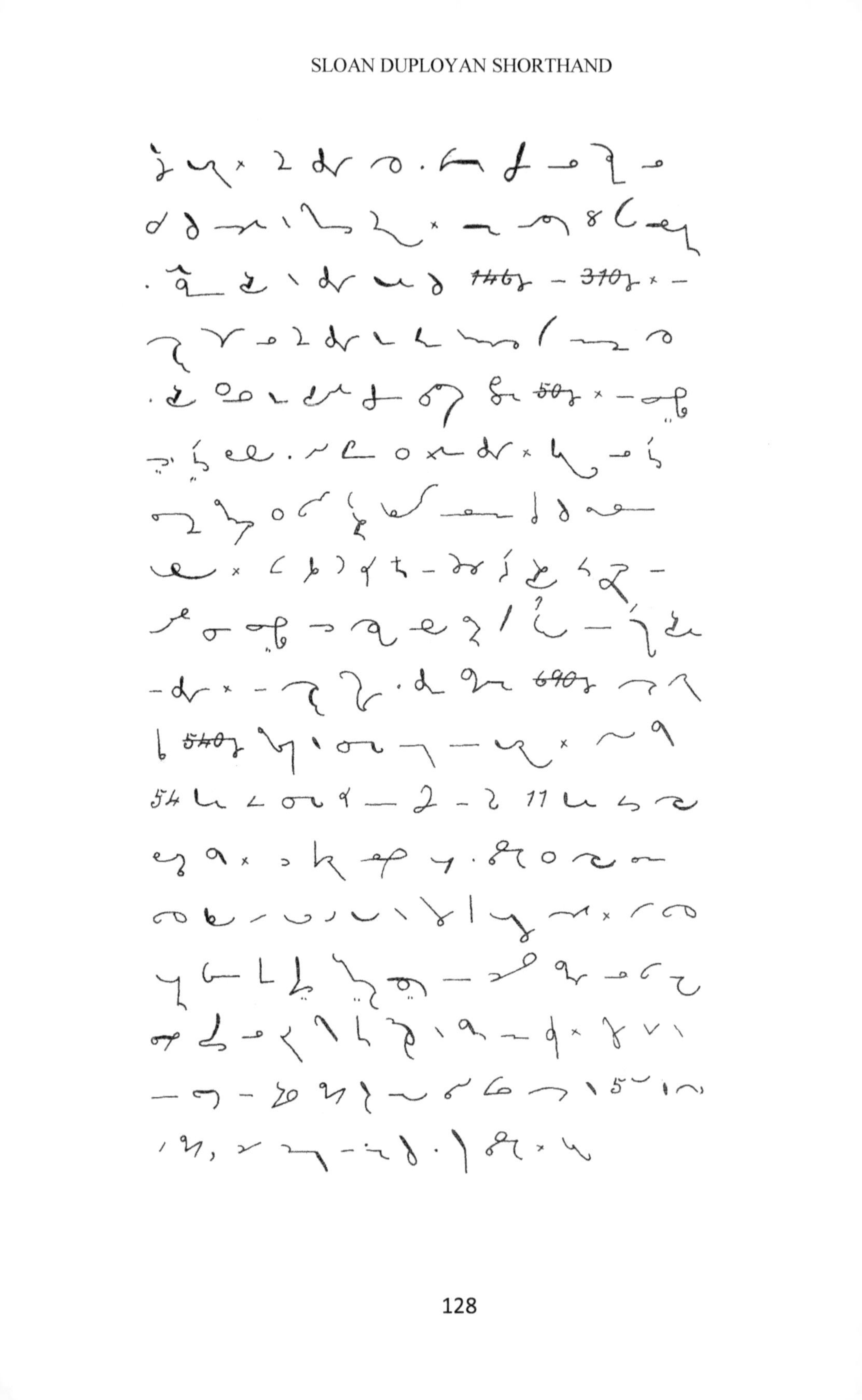

internal reserve. Net profits show a wonderful growth and a stability that comes from dealing in every day nests. During the last 8 years there has been an uninterrupted increase in profits rising from 146000 pounds to 310000 pounds. The charming status is that net profits for the current financial year to date show an increase over those for the corresponding period of last year of more than 50000 pounds. The Uthopia Tea Company has also a long record of excellent profits. Previously that company had a net advantage of its own manufacturing in accepts and had to be a form house had sources. With practice no capital expenditure to national company's factories can take over the supply of the Uthopia Tea Shops, those affecting great economies and considerably increasing the profits. The Chairman estimates a profit of not less than 690000 pounds which would leave about 540000 pounds available for ordinary and have do reserves. This is over 54 percent on the ordinary capital and equal to nearly 11 percent on these shares as now offered. We believe that those would seek an allotment of shares at the issue price will see them rise in the value by several shillings. This issue is being made by the Barkley Investment Trust and we are of the opinion that its terms attract security that they have ever been instrumental in offering to the public. If you will fill in and return the enclosed application form to us along with your cheque for 5 shilling per share on application we will endeavour to obtain for you a variable allotment. Yours faithfully

Dear Sir, in reply to your inquiry of yesterday we confidently recommend a new issue of 7 ½ percent cumulative preference share of 1 pound each and ordinary shares of 10 shilling each in Waverly Picture Productions Ltd. For each 10 preference shares allotted, you have the right that allotment of one ordinary share of 10 shilling at par by applications for ordinary shares alone will not be accepted. Without doubt I have a substantial premium will be bid for these ordinary shares as soon as the market commences. This company is unique in this country and it amalgamates film producers, film distributors, and also 20 picture theatres, including some of the best noon cinemas in London. The dividend on the 7 ½ percent preference shares is covered over 3 times. Very large distributions can be safely anticipated on the ordinary shares which now show near 20 percent. The profits for the current year are expected to exceed those of last year. This company is a combination of the best British interests in the cinema trade and is in a position to produce and exhibit to assist standard of film at/right. The importance of this new company is indicated by the many verbal references in the newspapers during the last

few days. Enormous profits are made from successive films and although the profits shown in the prospectus are excellent, there is every likelihood of very much better results in the future. We consider that you need not have any hesitation in investing the entire amount mentioned in your letter. We are Sir, Yours faithfully.

-x-

METHODS

Figuring Out **Ult. and Inst.** in a Date (frequently came in this book)

BY AMY JOHNSON CROW

You found your ancestor's obituary. Yay! There's just one problem. It says that he died "on the 5th inst." Or what about that marriage announcement you found? The happy couple got married "on the 27th ult." They sort of look like dates, but what are "inst" and "ult"?

Ult. and inst. are abbreviations that refer to months, but in a relative way. Let's take a look.

Inst. = Instant = Current Month

Inst. is an abbreviation for instant, which refers to the "present or current month," according to Merriam-Webster.

G. W. Spurgeon obituary, (Topeka) Kansas Farmer, 17 December 1879. Newspapers.com.

G.W. Spurgeon died "on the 3rd inst." That alone doesn't give us enough information to know which month it refers to. We need to know when this obituary was published.

The obituary appeared in the Kansas Farmer on 17 December 1879. Since "inst." refers to the present or current month, Spurgeon died 3 December 1879.

Ult. = Ultimo = Previous Month

Ult. is short for ultimo, meaning "of or occurring in the month preceding the present." Like inst., we can't know which month it's referring to unless we know what the "present" month is.

Brooklyn Daily Eagle, 7 August 1900. Newspapers.com.

Ult. can trip us up. When we read that Pvt. Guy De St. Croix died "5th ult." and the article is datelined 7 August, it's easy to think he died 5 August. He actually died 5 July. Ult. refers to the month preceding the present. The article is in August, so the month preceding would be July. (If he had died in August, he would have died "5th inst.")

Month's Name

January

February

March

April

May

June

July

August

September

October

November

December

Name of Days

Sunday

Monday

Tuesday

Wednesday

Thursday

friday

Saturday

www.ingramcontent.com/pod-product-compliance
Lightning Source LLC
Chambersburg PA
CBHW041330120726
48005CB00014B/2193